PALEO GRILLING

THE COMPLETE COOKBOOK

13-Digit ISBN: 9781604335385
10-Digit ISBN: 1604335386

This book may be ordered by mail from the publisher. Please include $5.95 for postage and handling.

Please support your local bookseller first!

Books published by Cider Mill Press Book Publishers are available at special discounts for bulk purchases in the United States by corporations, institutions, and other organizations. For more information, please contact the publisher.

Cider Mill Press Book Publishers
"Where good books are ready for press"
12 Spring St.
PO Box 454
Kennebunkport, Maine 04046

Visit us on the Web!
www.cidermillpress.com

Design by Jon Chaiet
All images used under license from Shutterstock.com.

Printed in China

1 2 3 4 5 6 7 8 9 0

First Edition

PALEO GRILLING

THE COMPLETE COOKBOOK

FROM RIBS TO RUBS
TO SIZZLING SIDES,
EVERYTHING YOU NEED
FOR YOUR PALEO BBQ

JOHN WHALEN III

WITH CONTRIBUTIONS FROM
JOHN F. WHALEN JR.

CIDER MILL PRESS

BOOK
PUBLISHERS

KENNEBUNKPORT, MAINE

Contents

Why Paleo and Grilling Are a Match Made in Heaven

BY SONIA LACASSE OF THEHEALTHYFOODIE.COM

If you ask me to describe the Paleo lifestyle in a few simple words, this is what immediately comes to mind: eat real food, and keep it clean and simple. The word "meat" follows soon after. It's no secret that the inclusion of good quality, well-sourced meat as the main source of protein in your diet is one of the core principles of the Paleo lifestyle.

For most of my life, I have been what I humorously referred to as a Hard-Corus Humanus Carnivorous. I really, really love my meat. But I almost gave it up entirely and embraced vegetarianism, convinced that cutting out meat and fats would help lead me down a healthier path. That was until I decided to take a thirty-day clean eating challenge that removed any and all forms of grains, dairy, refined sugar, and processed food from my diet—I ate nothing but meat, healthy fats, vegetables, some fruits, and a few nuts and seeds.

Little did I know that this, in a nutshell, is what the Paleo diet is all about... and I'd just gotten completely hooked on it!

For me, this new lifestyle has proven to be a total liberation: no more calorie and macro counting, no more eating small, unsatisfying meals at regular intervals, no more staying slightly hungry all the time, no more stepping on the scale every week and obsessing over that number—I felt liberated and felt so much better physically, too! My all too familiar migraines soon became a thing of the past, and my skin is glowing, as if by miracle.

Not only that, but I found that the Paleo lifestyle opened up a whole new world of possibilities for me in the kitchen, now that my beloved meat had been reinstated and now that I realized that fat was not the enemy—it's what kept me full and satisfied. I felt inspired to come up with new, tasty, and healthy Paleo recipes nearly every day.

From that point on, I started researching the diet more extensively and soon came to realize that the source of your food is almost as important as the food itself: Whatever your food eats, you end up eating, too. Same goes for what ends up on your food, and where your food is grown: It all ends up in your body. The way I see it, the Paleo diet is all about feeding on the highest possible quality of plants and animals that you can find or afford, and filling your plate with food from sustainable sources that has undergone as little processing as possible.

These principles truly walk hand in hand with the clean and simple cooking method of grilling your food. Paleo-friendly foods include meat, fish and seafood, eggs, tons of fresh vegetables as well as some fruit, nuts, and seeds. See? It's about much more than just fatty cuts of meat. Just like the grill!

Most people think of a grill as a means of cooking meat and nothing else. It's true that I can't imagine a better association than that of meat to grill; they're simply a match made in heaven.

But grilling is also an extraordinary, convenient and healthy way to cook vegetables and even fruits. Most of the time you can get away with a simple little brushing of olive oil and a sprinkle of salt and pepper. The flames will take care of bringing the flavor to the next level for you.

And the best part is there will be so few dishes to clean!

So light up that grill and experience your food in its purest form—and most tantalizing flavor!

What Is the Paleo Diet, and Why Is It Good for Me?

BY DOMINIQUE DEVITO

First, congratulations on your interest in the Paleo diet. You'll soon learn that going Paleo is about more than just diet, though it certainly starts there. It's also about making choices for a healthier lifestyle all around. And that's wonderful.

Like any bold change you want to make to better your health, this one will require some sacrifices and will take some getting used to. This may sound discouraging, but it's important to be honest. The Paleo plan requires that you give up foods that you may have learned to associate with comfort and good times, like sugar, white bread and potatoes, processed foods, and dairy. I know, it sounds scary. The good news—and it's really good news!—is that the sacrifices you'll make have huge payoffs for your health. Within the first few weeks of making the change to the Paleo diet, you should experience:

INCREASED ENERGY • MODERATE WEIGHT LOSS • IMPROVED DIGESTION • IMPROVED SKIN TONE AND HAIR CONDITION • IMPROVED MOOD, INCLUDING MORE RESTFUL SLEEP

If these are the benefits you're seeking, you won't be disappointed.

What Is Paleo?

"Paleo" is short for Paleolithic. This was the time period dating from approximately 2 million to 12,000 BCE. Next was the Mesolithic Era, from roughly 12,000 to 8,000 BCE, and the Neolithic Era, or 8,000 to approximately 5,000 BCE and the transition to a more agricultural, domestic lifestyle for ancient humans. The Paleolithic era is also referred to as the Stone Age. It is when our ancestors became much more skilled at hunting with stone tools, which enabled them to hunt animals more effectively. For most of this period, humans were simple hunter-gatherers, competing for food sources with the likes of wooly mammoths and savage wooly rhinoceroses, giant deer, bison, musk ox, and hare. They were much more in synch with their environments—out of necessity—and adapted to the demands of the day, spending many hours foraging and hunting.

Because caves afforded some of the best protection against the wildlife and the elements, we have come to refer to our ancestors of these eras as "cavemen," and thus the Paleo(lithic) diet

is sometimes referred to as the caveman diet. It is a simplification, of course, but it also provides a great concept for the diet, which is one based largely on meat, fish, eggs, vegetables, and fruits. It's also a fitting concept for the lifestyle of Paleo people—active, ever watchful, keenly aware of their surroundings.

Paleo for the Modern World

Though we may be borrowing from the concept of "necessity" eating and activity from our Paleo brethren (and sistren), be glad we are living in today's modern world where, for us, this is a choice rather than a necessity. If we had to get out there and bring down our meals on a regular basis, we wouldn't have time to read—or write—

cookbooks such as these! We've come a long way, baby—for real!—and there's no need to go backward. That's another great thing about today's Paleo diet (and this cookbook): It contains far more variety than a caveperson could have ever conceived of, and healthier means of preparation, as well!

Another consideration for the modern Paleo is the very real awareness of the impact of domesticated meat production on the planet. Cavemen weren't killing herds of black Angus beef cattle; they were taking on animals in the wild. And the caveman population wasn't at nearly 7 billion worldwide. If everyone went Paleo, the increased demand for domesticated meat could do more harm than good on a global level. These are discussion points beyond the scope of this cookbook but ones that Paleo enthusiasts debate frequently, and rightly so.

As the benefits of the diet to their overall health make them even greater supporters of it, they explore more and more of its aspects. One of the founding fathers of the Paleo diet and lifestyle is Loren Cordain, PhD. He is the author of *The Paleo Diet* and several spinoffs from that book. He speaks about the diet around the world. He has a website (www.the paleodiet.com) and a blog and is considered "the leading expert on Paleolithic diets and founder of the paleo movement." He is an excellent resource to tap into as you learn more about all things Paleo.

Don't Just Go Paleo, Go Local!

A clean eating trend that dovetails with the Paleo lifestyle is the commitment to eating "local." Environmental and economic benefits aside, participating in the increasingly popular "locavore lifestyle" helps guarantee that the food you're putting in your body is as fresh as it could possibly be and that it's free of chemical preservatives. It makes sense: If you seek out produce from local farmers, farm stands, or farmers' markets, the minimal amount of travel time required to get the food from farm to table (as opposed to produce that has to cross an ocean to get to your kitchen) makes it possible to transport fresh crops, as opposed to chemically preserved ones. And if you think about it, our Paleolithic ancestors likely didn't travel very far to find their food, so we shouldn't either—if we can manage it! Luckily, eating local is easier than ever these days: According to the U.S. Department of Agriculture, the number of small farms has increased by about 20 percent over the past six years, making local produce and locally raised meat more accessible than ever. It's a great time to go Paleo!

Your Paleo Pantry

At its core, the Paleo diet demands that you remove grains, dairy, legumes, sugar, and all processed foods from your diet, focusing instead on consuming fresh, locally sourced meat, fish, fruits, vegetables, nuts, and seeds as much as possible. There are some gray areas in terms of some foods that are considered acceptable for the Paleo diet for various reasons, and this cookbook has decided to include the following ingredients in our grilling recipes, for the reasons specified below:

Butter: While dairy should be avoided for anyone adhering to the Paleo diet, we've made an exception for small quantities of grass-fed clarified butter (ghee), especially when it's locally sourced. It's true that our Paleolithic ancestors didn't consume butter in the form that we encounter it today, but when the proteins and sugars are removed and only the pure butter fat, or "clarified butter" remains, we're left with a saturated fat that's similar to the healthy saturated fats we find in animals.

Oil: If you stick to non-hydrogenated, extra-virgin oils, like coconut oil and olive oil (as opposed to artificial oils like vegetable oil and canola oil), you're in the clear!

Peas (and green beans): While legumes are strictly outlawed on the Paleo diet, we've made

> **TIP:** IF YOU LIVE IN AN URBAN AREA WHERE FARM-FRESH MEAT AND PRODUCE CAN BE HARD TO FIND, THINK ABOUT JOINING A CSA— THIS STANDS FOR COMMUNITY SUPPORTED AGRICULTURE, OR COMMUNITY SHARED AGRICULTURE. WHEN YOU JOIN, YOU RECEIVE A "SHARE" OF FRESH PRODUCE DELIVERED ON A REGULAR BASIS FROM LOCAL FARMS. LEARN MORE ABOUT CSAs AND FIND TIPS FOR CHOOSING A CSA AT HTTP://WWW.LOCALHARVEST.ORG/CSA/

an exception for peas and green beans, as have many Paleo enthusiasts. Peas are picked fresh before they dry—and eaten fresh—unlike most other legumes, which are allowed to dry on the vine and contain a high-carbohydrate content, making other legumes not too dissimilar from grains.

Vinegar: Apple cider and coconut vinegars are acceptable, but make sure you're not using varieties that are overly processed, flavored, or contain other artificial sweeteners and added ingredients that aren't Paleo.

Wine: Alcohol is off-limits when it comes to the Paleo diet—most alcoholic beverages are made from grains, and many are also filled with sugars and artificial flavors. Plus, most alcohols are notorious gut irritants. However, we've decided to make an exception for organic wine—especially red wine—when consumed in small quantities. The ingredient at its core—grapes—is a Paleo-friendly food, and the health benefits of the antioxidants in wine make occasional consumption acceptable in many Paleo communities.

Keep reading for more tips on stocking a Paleo pantry, in case you're going to take your dedication to the Paleo movement beyond just the grill. But be warned: Going Paleo begins with a "pantry purge."

Stocking a Paleo Pantry Starts with Emptying Your Cupboards!

BY DOMINIQUE DEVITO

Out Before In

Get started by finding a sturdy cardboard box or some of your larger recyclable grocery bags, as you want to be able to pack up the intact packages of foods won't be needing anymore and easily take them to a family member, friend, or your local food pantry.

Start with your pantry. You want to remove any grains—rice of any kind, pasta, noodles, quinoa, oatmeal, and so forth.

You'll also want to purge your shelves of any foods that include sugar. Read the labels if you're uncertain, as this includes any artificial sweeteners, as well, and there are many of them. Some of the more common are saccharine, aspartame, sucralose, corn syrup, and high fructose corn syrup.

Next, remove any containers of processed oils—vegetable oil, canola oil, and peanut oil are some of the more popular. Anything that is hydrogenated or partially hydrogenated has to go. Don't worry; fats are a necessary part of a Paleo diet and good health, and there are several on the "must-have" list.

While vegetables are a major component of the Paleo diet, legumes are off limits, as they contain anti-nutrients and contribute to digestive distress and bloating. Legumes include most types of beans, including kidney, garbanzo, pinto, fava, and soy. (We're allowing peas and green beans; see page 11.)

Move on to your refrigerator and freezer. Say goodbye to dairy—milk, butter or margarine, cheese, yogurt, ice cream. Say goodbye to bottled salad dressings, deli meats, juices, and anything that contains nitrates, sweeteners, artificial ingredients, or other non-Paleo ingredients, as mentioned above.

To summarize, here's what you want to get out of your kitchen:

• PASTAS AND OTHER GRAINS • OATMEAL • BREAKFAST CEREALS • GRANOLA • RICE • BREADS, CRACKERS, CHIPS • SUGAR, INCLUDING BROWN, LIGHT BROWN, AND CONFECTIONER'S • ARTIFICIAL SWEETENERS, AND PRODUCTS THAT CONTAIN THEM • CANDY, COOKIES • VEGETABLE OIL • CANOLA OIL • PEANUT OIL • SUNFLOWER OIL • CORN OIL • SOYBEAN OIL •

SHORTENING • PEANUT BUTTER, MIXED NUTS (ESPECIALLY COCKTAIL PEANUTS) • CANS OR BAGS OF BEANS—RED, KIDNEY, PINTO, LIMA, GARBANZO • JAMS AND JELLIES • SALAD DRESSINGS • SOY SAUCE • PACKAGED SAUCES OR CONDIMENTS, INCLUDING KETCHUP AND MUSTARD • MILK, BUTTER, CREAM, MARGARINE, YOGURT, ICE CREAM, AND OTHER DAIRY

Now heed this advice: Take away the foods you've removed immediately! You do not want to be tempted by any of them!

In and Begin

Once you've removed the no-no's, it's time to stock up on what will become the staples of your new, healthier diet. Besides referencing the lists here, browse through this cookbook and take note of ingredients that sound especially good. Remember, one of the main reasons that a Paleo diet can be so healthy for you is that it is focused on fresher, more easily digested food sources. When considering what to stock up on, always think fresh.

Be forewarned: Your body will go through cravings for foods you once took for granted—especially those with sugar—and you'll want to be sure you have the makings of something really tasty so you can feel good about your decision and stick with your commitment.

For the Cupboard

Most of your ancillary ingredients on the Paleo diet will be seasonings, as the essentials are truly simple: meat, fish, eggs, vegetables, fruits, and berries. Depending on how old some of your current seasonings are, you may want to start fresh. Stock up on seasonings so you have lots of options when it's time to cook. And while it's important to have a great selection of seasonings, remember that fresher is always better, so use fresh herbs when you can.

Stock Up On:

- Dried herbs, including parsley, oregano, chives, mint, basil, thyme, tarragon, sage, bay leaves, and rosemary
- Ground spices, including cayenne pepper, cumin, coriander, ginger, nutmeg, clove, curry powder, allspice, paprika, chili powder, mustard, and cardamom
- Pepper and iodized sea salt

There are all kinds of spice combinations on the market today, and almost all are fair game for Paleo cooking. Just be sure to read the ingredients and make sure they don't contain artificial sweeteners or preservatives.

Oils and Other Staples

Your pantry will look woefully bare without cans and jars and containers of beans, jams, cereals, pasta, spaghetti sauces, and snacks. Yikes! Time to move in what's Paleo-approved:

- Oils contribute necessary fats to a diet and are essential for cooking. Those that can be used for a Paleo diet are extra-virgin olive oil, coconut oil (unrefined), avocado oil, nut oils (like walnut or almond), and seed oils (flax and sesame, for example).
- Dried fruits, which make for great snacks—in moderation and with no additional sweetener added.
- Dry or roasted nuts, like almonds, walnuts, pistachios, and cashews. Again, in moderation.
- Broths and stocks, including chicken, beef

and vegetable broths, so long as there are no sugars or soy in them.

- Vinegars, including apple cider and coconut.
- Olives packed in water with minimal salt.
- Pickles jarred without sugars or chemicals.
- Canned fish packed in water or olive oil (not soybean oil), including tuna, salmon, and sardines.
- Tomato paste and salsa without added sugar, corn or wheat.
- Fish sauce.
- Coconut aminos (a soy-free seasoning sauce that's loaded with amino acids).

Protein Sources

Proteins comprise the bulk of the Paleo diet, so it's important to shop smart for what is healthiest. For meats like beef, lamb, and pork, you want to be sure you're purchasing grass-fed, organically raised sources. Poultry should be free-range. The best fish is wild-caught. Cold-water, oily fishes like herring, anchovies, mackerel, salmon, and sardines are the highest in omega-3 fatty acids.

The most economical way to stock up on meats and fish is to buy in bulk if possible. Find a farmer at a farmers' market whose meats meet with your approval, and discuss purchasing a side of an animal. It may be worth investing in a freezer to accommodate this quantity, as it is definitely more economical in the long run.

The Paleo diet includes high-quality sources of: **BEEF • PORK • LAMB • POULTRY • EGGS • FISH AND SEAFOOD • GAME MEATS (PHEASANT, BOAR, BEAR, ELK, ETC.)**

Remember, too, that organ meats (liver, kidneys, brain, etc.) were a true Paleo staple (and often the highest-prized cuts), so be sure to keep these in your freezer. Slow cooking is a great way to mellow out some of the pungency in these cuts, making them as tender and flavorful as traditional cuts.

Vegetables

There are three words to describe stocking up on this part of the Paleo diet: Go for it!

The only items you'll need to avoid in the produce section of your grocery store—or at the farmers' market—are corn and white potatoes. So whether your tastes run to leafy greens, crunchy carrots, zucchini, squashes, cabbage and Brussels sprouts, asparagus, beets, or artichokes—indulge in them and enjoy.

Fruits and Berries

As you transition to Paleo, if you've been used to ending your meals with a sweet treat, the sugar monster will haunt you. It will seem like everywhere you look there are sweet foods that you can't eat, from a decadent fruit-topped cheesecake to an itty-bitty dark chocolate chip.

To help beat back the sugar monster, be sure you have fruits and berries with you at all times. Keep a small bag of dried fruit in the car or in your desk drawer (just make sure there's no added sugar). If you crave something soft and sweet, turn to a ripe banana, which you can get almost any time of year.

Just as most vegetables are Paleo-acceptable, the same is true of fruits. You can enjoy oranges, apples, tangerines, strawberries, raspberries, peaches, pineapples, grapes, watermelon, and cantaloupe.

Smoke and Fire

What's more primal than fire?

The Paleo diet gets its inspiration from the Paleolithic era, when our ancestors were hunter-gatherers who would huddle around a fire, delighting in the aroma of roasting meat, eggs, vegetables, and fruits.

Today, some of the healthiest, most delicious meals are just fancier, more convenient replications of those outdoor feasts. At the heart, it's still about fresh, local ingredients cooked with fire and seasoned with smoke.

Today's Paleo grilling enthusiast has a plethora of choices, not only when it comes to food sources but regarding what equipment is used. You can use a fancy gas grill with temperature dials, or use charcoal or wood. You can cook in a Dutch oven over white coals (Grilled Seafood Stew in Tomato Broth, page 250). You can use a cast-iron skillet to grill main dishes as well as wide variety of sides and sauces, from Chorizo-Stuffed Mushrooms (page 27) to Basil-Walnut Pesto (page 234). Skewers are ideal for grilling small pieces of meat—the essence of kebabs—as well as shrimp, vegetables, and fresh fruit. And twine can hold things together—like a bunch of Bacon-Wrapped Asparagus (page 238)—over the grates. The recipes in this book use all these methods. We even grill a whole butterflied chicken under a brick wrapped in aluminum foil (Chicken Under Brick with Cilantro Oil, page 196).

Many of our recipes say the grill is ready when it's about 450 degrees with the coals lightly covered in ash. Another way to gauge that temperature is to hold your hand about 5 inches above the grates. If you can only hold it there 1 to 3 seconds (don't get all caveman macho!), the grill is at the medium-hot temperature we desire.

Only one fuel adds flavor: Wood. Sometimes we suggest you go for a smoky flavor by adding woodchips to your electric or gas grill. Wood chips burn quickly, making them great for smoking smaller pieces of meat, like chicken breasts, steak, or sausages. For example, in our recipe for Leg of Lamb with Rosemary-Mustard Marinade (page 144), we soak 2 to 3 cups of hickory or oak woodchips an hour before cooking, scatter them over the coals, and cover the grill so that the smoke pillows around the meat. This really brings out the mustard flavor.

But if you want to smoke a large piece for a longer time, wood chunks—or even larger split logs!—make more sense. My dad introduces the Beef chapter with a story about grilling a couple of delicious porterhouses over a handmade Mexican clay fire pit, using some scavenged wood.

He taught me the art of grilling—the balance between the cut of meat, the temperature of the flame or coals, and the quality of the smoke—and timing it all just right. And when it all comes together, it's about far more than sustenance, far more than abiding by the rules of a particular diet. It's perfection.

Starters

Starters are often forgotten when it comes to a family dinners and gatherings. While appetizers are traditionally served in small portions before the main course, they are in no way something that should be left out. Always packed with flavor, starters pave the way for the perfect grilled dish. As we have found, grilled appetizers always seem to be both the most hearty dishes as well as the most snacked on. Complemented by grilling's smoky atmosphere and warming aromas, these appetizers work perfectly as snacks for your guests while you work on the main dish.

Our starters include Grilled Calamari (page 38), Beefsteak Tomatoes with Basil and Balsamic Vinaigrette (page 35), and Shrimp Cocktail (page 33). In addition, we've also added new twists on old classics, including Bacon Deviled Eggs (page 34) and Chorizo-Stuffed Mushrooms (page 27). As always, don't hesitate to add some of your own inspirations on the recipes!

Classic Buffalo Wings

MAKES 4 TO 6 SERVINGS • ACTIVE TIME: 15 MINUTES • TOTAL TIME: 2 HOURS AND 30 MINUTES

Perfect for a Sunday with the boys, this dish never gets old. For this recipe, I decided to add a smoky flavor to the wings by adding a couple cups of pre-soaked hickory or oak woodchips to the coals. This style is optional, though I strongly recommend it.

1. Place the chicken wings on a roasting pan and put in the refrigerator. Let rest for at least 2 hours so that the skin on the wings tightens, promoting a crisp wing.

2. One hour before grilling, add the woodchips into a bowl of water and let soak.

3. A half hour before grilling, prepare your gas or charcoal grill to high heat.

4. In a small saucepan, add the clarified butter over medium heat. When hot, add the garlic and cook until golden—about 2 minutes. Next, mix in all of the remaining ingredients and bring to a simmer of medium heat. Simmer for about 3 minutes and then remove from heat and place in a large bowl.

5. Remove the chicken wings from the refrigerator and toss with the buffalo sauce in the large bowl.

6. When the grill is ready, at about 450 degrees with the coals lightly covered with ash, scatter the woodchips over the coals and then place the chicken wings on the grill with a good amount of space between them. Cover the grill and cook for about 2 to 3 minutes on each side, frequently basting each wing with the remaining buffalo sauce. Remove from grill when the skin is crispy.

7. Place on a large serving platter and serve warm alongside celery.

TOOLS

2 to 3 cups hickory or oak woodchips

INGREDIENTS

2 pounds chicken wings, split

2 tablespoons clarified butter

3 garlic cloves, minced

¼ teaspoon cayenne

¼ teaspoon paprika

2 teaspoons Tabasco

¼ cup Frank's Cayenne Pepper Sauce

1 head celery, stalks cut into 3-inch pieces

Chorizo-Stuffed Mushrooms

MAKES 8 TO 10 SERVINGS • ACTIVE TIME: 25 MINUTES • TOTAL TIME: 50 MINUTES

These chorizo-stuffed mushrooms can be very filling so try not to eat too many of them. The Spanish chorizo has a strong spice to it and pairs well with a glass of red wine.

1. Prepare your gas or charcoal grill to medium heat. Leave a cast-iron skillet on the grill while heating so that it develops a faint, smoky flavor.

2. While waiting, add the chorizo into a food processor and puree into a thick paste. Remove and set aside.

3. When the grill is ready, at about 350 to 400 degrees with the coals lightly covered with ash, brush the mushroom caps with the 2 tablespoons of olive oil. Next, place the mushroom tops on the grill and cook for about 2 minutes until the tops have browned. Remove from grill and place on a baking sheet.

4. Next, add the remaining ¼ cup of olive oil to the cast-iron skillet, followed by the onion and cherry tomatoes. Cook until the onion is translucent, about 2 minutes, and then stir in the pureed chorizo. Continue to cook until the chorizo is lightly browned, about 3 minutes, and then add in the chicken broth and parsley. Cook for only a minute or so longer, and then remove from heat.

5. Using a spoon, add the chorizo mixture into the mushroom caps. Move the baking sheet to a cool side of the grill and cook for about 15 minutes until the chorizo has browned. Remove from the grill, season with coarsely ground black pepper and fresh sea salt, and serve hot.

TOOLS
Cast-iron skillet
Food processor
Baking sheet

INGREDIENTS
1 Spanish chorizo, casing removed
14 white mushrooms, stemmed
¼ cup, plus 2 tablespoons olive oil
1 medium white onion, finely chopped
4 cherry tomatoes, quartered
¼ cup chicken broth
1 small bunch parsley, finely chopped
Coarsely ground black pepper
Fresh sea salt

Jalapeños Filled with Sausage and Diced Tomatoes

MAKES 5 TO 6 SERVINGS • ACTIVE TIME: 20 MINUTES • TOTAL TIME: 1 HOUR

Grilled stuffed jalapeños are simple and quick to prepare. Although the jalapeños are considered a hot pepper, when you seed and grill them, their heat is toned down and softer. For the sausage, if you are looking to save some time, pick up organic pork sausage (from a local butcher, if possible). It never fails!

1. Prepare your gas or charcoal grill to medium heat. Leave a cast-iron skillet on the grill while heating so that it develops a faint, smoky flavor.

2. When the grill is ready, at about 350 to 400 degrees with the coals lightly covered with ash, heat the olive oil in the skillet and then add the pork sausage. Cook until the sausage is no longer pink but evenly brown.

3. When the sausage is near complete, add the garlic and onion and cook until translucent, about 2 to 3 minutes. Stir in the red bell peppers and the cherry tomatoes and cook for another 2 minutes or so. Transfer the sausage stuffing from the grill and let rest.

4. Arrange the halves of the jalapeño peppers evenly on a baking sheet. Using a spoon, add the sausage mixture into the cavities of the peppers. Transfer to the grill and cook, covered, for about 20 minutes until lightly browned. Remove from the grill, season with pepper and salt, and serve immediately.

VARIATION After filling the jalapeños with the sausage mixture, wrap each jalapeño halve with a thick cut of bacon. Using a toothpick, pierce each wrapped jalapeño through its middle so that the bacon doesn't unravel while grilling. Grill for about 20 minutes until the bacon is crisp and browned.

TOOLS

Cast-iron skillet

Baking sheet

2 tablespoons olive oil

1 pound pork sausage

2 garlic cloves, minced

¼ small red onion, minced

3 tablespoons minced red bell pepper

8 cherry tomatoes, minced

12 to 16 jalapeno peppers, halved and seeded

Coarsely ground black pepper

Fresh sea salt

Smoked Spiced Chicken Wings

MAKES 4 TO 6 SERVINGS • ACTIVE TIME: 30 MINUTES • TOTAL TIME: 3 HOURS

These chicken wings are great for warm summer evenings with friends.
I recommend serving alongside celery and some Shishito Peppers (page 260).

TOOLS

2 to 3 cups hickory or oak woodchips

INGREDIENTS

2 pounds chicken wings, split

2 tablespoons olive oil

½ small lime, juiced

3 garlic cloves, finely chopped

2 tablespoons flat-leaf parsley, finely chopped

1 tablespoon ground cumin

2 teaspoons paprika

1 teaspoon ground cinnamon

1 teaspoon turmeric

1 teaspoon red pepper flakes

½ teaspoon onion powder

Coarsely ground black pepper

Fresh sea salt

1. Place the chicken wings on a roasting pan and put in the refrigerator. Let rest for at least 2 hours so that the skin on the wings tightens, promoting a crisp wing.

2. One hour before grilling, add the woodchips into a bowl of water and let soak.

3. A half hour before grilling, prepare your gas or charcoal grill to high heat.

4. While the grill heats, remove the wings from the refrigerator and add to a large bowl. Toss with the 2 tablespoons of olive oil.

5. In a medium bowl, combine all of the remaining ingredients.

6. Next, add the seasoning into the large bowl of chicken wings and toss evenly, making sure that each wing has an equal amount of seasoning.

7. When the grill is ready, at about 450 degrees with the coals lightly covered with ash, scatter the woodchips over the coals and then place the chicken wings on the grill with a good amount of space between them. Cover the grill and cook for about 2 to 3 minutes on each side. Remove from grill when the skin is crispy. Serve immediately.

Classic Antipasti

MAKES 4 SERVINGS • ACTIVE TIME: 15 MINUTES • TOTAL TIME: 1 HOUR

This dish is best served for large family gatherings. As this is just a base recipe, feel free to add more ingredients if you would like!

12 cherry tomatoes

½ cup, plus 4 tablespoons olive oil

½ cup assorted olives

½ teaspoon garlic, chopped

1 sprig thyme, leaves removed

¼ cup walnuts

¼ cup almonds

½ pound fresh prosciutto, shaved

8 to 10 thick slices hard salami

Coarsely ground black pepper

1. Stem the cherry tomatoes and place in a small bowl. Submerge in a high-quality olive oil and let marinate for 30 minutes to 1 hour.

2. In a small bowl, mix the assorted olives, garlic, thyme, and remaining 2 tablespoons of olive oil and let marinate for 30 minutes to 1 hour.

3. Take a small frying pan and place it over medium-high heat. Add in 2 tablespoons of olive oil. When hot, stir in the walnuts and almonds and toast for about 2 minutes. Remove and set aside.

4. Arrange the prosciutto and hard salami on a large platter and garnish/season lightly with coarsely cracked black pepper.

5. Arrange the almonds, tomatoes, and olives on the platter as well. Serve immediately.

Shrimp Cocktail

MAKES 10 TO 12 SERVINGS • ACTIVE TIME: 10 MINUTES • TOTAL TIME: 1 HOUR AND 30 MINUTES

This is a classic summer dish. Most cocktail sauces include ketchup, but you can never be sure about what ingredients are and are not Paleo in store-bought kinds. With that in mind, here we start with a tomato-sauce foundation, and then build upon that to arrive at a fresh and original cocktail sauce. Enjoy this chilled, perhaps with a glass of white wine.

1. Arrange the pre-cooked shrimp on a large platter and place in the refrigerator. Chill for at least 1 hour before serving.

2. In a medium bowl, mix all of the ingredients except for the quartered lemon. Place in the refrigerator and chill for about 30 minutes.

3. Place the bowl of the cocktail sauce, along with the wedges of lemon, in the center of the shrimp platter. Serve chilled.

2 pounds pre-cooked shrimp, deveined and shells removed

16 ounces organic tomato sauce

1 to 2 tablespoons fresh horseradish, depending on your preference

1 teaspoon Dijon mustard

¼ small lemon, juiced

Coarsely ground black pepper

Fresh sea salt

1 large lemon, quartered

Bacon Deviled Eggs

MAKES 6 SERVINGS • ACTIVE TIME: 15 MINUTES • TOTAL TIME: 30 MINUTES

These are perfect for football Sundays. The recipe is very straightforward and is easy to adapt for a larger gathering. Keep in mind that this is a foundational recipe and you can take and add any other flavors that come to mind!

TOOLS

Food processor
Saucepan
Frying pan

INGREDIENTS

2 egg yolks, room temperature
¼ medium lemon, juiced
1 cup light olive oil
10 large eggs
6 thick strips of bacon
2 tablespoons Dijon mustard
2 tablespoons fresh parsley, finely chopped
Coarsely ground black pepper
Fresh sea salt
1 teaspoon paprika (optional)
3 chives, finely chopped (optional)

1. In a small food processor, add the 2 raw egg yolks and the lemon juice and puree for 30 seconds. Very gradually, add in the light olive oil until you reach a thick, mayonnaise-like consistency. It is extremely important to make sure that you add the light olive oil slowly to the processor, if you go too quickly, you will not reach the desired consistency.

2. Fill a medium saucepan with water. Carefully add the 10 eggs into the saucepan and then place the saucepan over medium heat. When the water reaches a boil, pull the eggs from the water and place under cool water. Let rest for a few minutes, and then peel back the shells.

3. Slice the eggs into halves. Using a fork, transfer the egg yolks from the eggs and place in a small bowl. Whisk in the Dijon mustard and parsley, and then season with coarsely ground black pepper and fresh sea salt. Set aside.

4. Place a medium frying pan over medium-high heat. Add the thick strips of bacon to the pan and cook until crispy, a few minutes on each side. (If you would like to add a smoked flavor to the bacon, consider smoking the bacon on the grill.) Transfer the bacon to a carving board and chop into bits. Whisk into the mixture.

5. Spoon the mixture from the small bowl back into the egg whites. If you would like, garnish with paprika and chopped chives. Serve chilled.

Beefsteak Tomatoes with Basil and Balsamic Vinaigrette

MAKES 4 TO 6 SERVINGS • ACTIVE TIME: 10 MINUTES • TOTAL TIME: 10 MINUTES

I recommend serving this before the main dish, as it is not too filling and offers the perfect level of flavor before the main course.

1. Place the beefsteak tomatoes on a platter, then layer with the basil leaves.

2. In a small glass, combine the olive oil and balsamic vinegar, and then spread it evenly across the tomatoes with basil.

3. Season with black pepper and sea salt, and then serve immediately.

4 beefsteak tomatoes, sliced into ½-inch pieces

½ cup fresh basil leaves

1 tablespoon olive oil

1 tablespoon balsamic vinegar

Coarsely ground black pepper

Fresh sea salt

Grilled Sardines with Lemon and Herbs

MAKES 6 SERVINGS • ACTIVE TIME: 15 MINUTES • TOTAL TIME: 40 MINUTES

The sardine is often considered to have one of the stronger "fish" flavor to it, and as such, be sure to serve these with a glass of white wine. For a garnish, serve with thin strips of lemon.

1. Line the bottom of a small baking dish with the sardines. Submerge the sardines with the fresh lemon juice and olive oil, and then transfer to the refrigerator. Let marinate for 30 minutes.

2. A half hour before grilling, prepare your gas or charcoal grill to medium-high heat.

3. While waiting, combine the garlic, shallot, parsley, and cilantro in a small bowl. Set next to the grill.

4. When the grill is ready, at about 400 degrees with the coals lightly covered with ash, remove the sardines from the refrigerator and place over direct heat. Season the tops of the sardines with the herb mixture, and then grill for about 1 to 2 minutes. Flip and season once more, cooking for 1 to 2 more minutes. Remove when the centers are opaque.

5. Transfer the sardines to a large carving board, and let rest for 5 minutes. Serve warm.

Fresh sardines, scaled, gutted and cleaned

2 large lemons, juiced

¼ cup olive oil

3 garlic cloves, finely chopped

1 small shallot, finely chopped

2 tablespoons flat-leaf parsley, finely chopped

1 tablespoon cilantro, finely chopped

Coarsely ground black pepper

Fresh sea salt

Grilled Calamari

MAKES 6 SERVINGS • ACTIVE TIME: 15 MINUTES • TOTAL TIME: 2 HOURS

Great as both an appetizer and a snack, grilled calamari goes best when served family style. As such, serve the calamari in a large dish and allow everyone to take what they like. Serve with marinara sauce (page 130).

TOOLS

Cast-iron skillet

INGREDIENTS

1 lemon, juiced

¼ cup olive oil

2 garlic cloves, finely chopped

2 sprigs fresh oregano, leaves removed

Coarsely ground black pepper

Fresh sea salt

2 pounds fresh squid, tentacles separated from bodies

1. Combine the lemon juice, olive oil, garlic, and oregano in a large bowl. Season with coarsely ground black pepper and fresh sea salt. Add the squid to the bowl and let marinate for 1 to 2 hours.

2. Prepare your gas or charcoal grill to medium-high heat. Leave a cast-iron skillet on the grill while heating so that it develops a faint, smoky flavor.

3. When the grill is ready, at about 400 degrees with the coals lightly covered with ash, place the squid tentacles and rings in the skillet and cook until opaque, about 3 to 4 minutes. When finished, transfer the squid to a large carving board and let stand at room temperature for 5 minutes before serving.

Soups *and* Salads

Soups and grilling are rarely paired together, but when they are they produce the best and most flavorful meals. Preparing soups over the grill will take time and frequent attention. When using a charcoal grill, that means restocking the coals about every hour. When making soups and salads on the grill, it is extremely important to find a quality charcoal that will give you the perfect mix between smoke and heat. In addition, be sure to have several cups of pre-soaked hickory or oak woodchips alongside the grill to toss onto the coals when needed.

There's just one secret to cooking soups and stews on the grill: a Dutch oven. The Dutch oven allows for a slow braising of the ingredients, while the cast iron will maintain a consistent heat and add to the flavoring; in fact, the more you use your cast-iron Dutch oven, the more flavors it will develop itself. Invest in a cast-iron Dutch oven from Le Creuset, Sur La Table, or any other leading brand. The Dutch oven will promote earthy dishes that will be best when made with the freshest ingredients over a long period of time.

Both the soups and salads in this chapter take advantage of the smoky flavors that come when grilling outdoors. You can't replicate real smoky flavor on a stovetop. There's nothing unsophisticated about our Portuguese Kale and Sausage Soup (page 47) or our Grilled Chicken Tomatillo Soup (page 63). We wanted to add real vintage flavors to our Smoked Tomato and Basil Soup (page 54) and Smoked Manhattan Clam Chowder (page 52), so our recipes require that you stoke the coals with hickory or oak woodchips. If you find that you need more smoke than the recipe already provides, cover the grill while cooking, aligning the air vent away from the Dutch oven so that the smoke pillows around the soup before escaping through the air vent.

Furthermore, the salads feature grilled ingredients and toppings that bring the flavors full circle. The salads in this chapter include Paleo toppings such as sunflower seeds toasted in a cast-iron skillet, fresh anchovy fillets for a classic Caesar salad, and char-grilled beets. Maple woodchips are perfect for bacon, as called for in our Frisée Salad with Maple-Smoked Bacon and Hard-Boiled Eggs (page 58) and our Sweet Potato Soup with Grilled Bacon and Walnuts (page 48).

Chicken Stock

MAKES ABOUT 12 CUPS • ACTIVE TIME: 11 HOURS • TOTAL TIME: 12 HOURS

We're starting with Chicken Stock—the base of not only so many soups but so many recipes in general. Stock can be stored in the refrigerator for several days, or kept frozen.

1. If you are using a whole chicken, cut off the neck, wings, and legs and cut them into pieces. Cut the rest of the chicken pieces into chunks.

2. Place a large Dutch oven on your gas or charcoal grill and prepare to medium heat. Leave the grill covered while heating, as it will add a faint smoky flavor to the Dutch oven.

3. When the grill is ready, at about 400 degrees with the coals lightly covered with ash, place the chicken pieces in the Dutch oven and top with all vegetables except the parsley. Cover with water and vinegar. Cover, and let the meat and vegetables cook in the liquid for 30 minutes to 1 hour.

4. Tending the coals every 30 minutes, cook for 2 to 3 hours, or until boiling. Remove the cover and spoon off and discard any "scum" that has risen to the top.

5. Replace the cover and reduce the grill to low-heat. Continue to add coals to the fire and cook for about 8 to 10 hours. Add the parsley in the last 15 minutes or so.

6. When cooking is complete, remove the solids with a slotted spoon into a colander over a bowl. Any drippings in the bowl can go back into the stock. Remove any meat from the bones and eat separately. Transfer the stock to a large bowl and refrigerate. When the fat is congealed on top, remove it, and transfer the stock to several smaller containers with tight-fitting lids.

VARIATION For a browner, even richer stock, place the chicken pieces on a cookie sheet. Preheat the oven broiler, and broil for about 3 minutes per side, until browned.

Made with all parts of the chicken, a slow-cooked stock is rich in many minerals essential to good health, including calcium, magnesium, phosphorous, silicon, sulphur, and even glucosamine and chondroitin.

1 whole free-range chicken, or 2 to 3 pounds of the bony parts (necks, backs, breastbones, legs, wings)

Gizzards from the chicken

2 to 4 chicken feet (optional but beneficial)

4 quarts cold water

2 tablespoons vinegar

1 large onion, chopped

2 carrots, peeled and sliced

2 celery stalks, chopped

1 bunch parsley, chopped

Classic Caesar Salad

MAKES 6 SERVINGS • ACTIVE TIME: 10 MINUTES • TOTAL TIME: 15 MINUTES

Anchovy filets are an essential ingredient to the Classic Caesar Salad—a Paleo favorite.

3 heads Romaine lettuce

2 garlic cloves, minced

½ small lemon, juiced

1 large egg

4 anchovy filets

1 teaspoon Dijon mustard

½ cup olive oil

Coarsely ground black pepper

Fresh sea salt

1. Rinse the heads of Romaine lettuce and then dry thoroughly. Place in refrigerator and set aside.

2. In a small bowl, whisk the minced garlic, lemon juice, and egg until blended. Whisk in the anchovy filets and Dijon mustard until the anchovies have been completely incorporated into the dressing.

3. Gradually whisk in the olive oil and then season with coarsely ground black pepper and sea salt. Place the dressing in the refrigerator for about 15 minutes and then pour over the chilled Romaine lettuce. Serve immediately.

VARIATION Top this salad with grilled chicken or smoked bacon.

Portuguese Kale and Sausage Soup

MAKES 6 SERVINGS • ACTIVE TIME: 45 MINUTES • TOTAL TIME: 1 HOUR

Sausage can be a hard Paleo-friendly meat to come by. However, if you were to go to your local farmers' market or butcher, you should be able to find homemade sausage that works for your diet. It will be worth it, especially in this traditional Portuguese soup.

1. Place a large Dutch oven on your gas or charcoal grill and prepare to medium heat. Leave the grill covered while heating, as it will add a faint smoky flavor to the skillet.

2. When the grill is ready, at about 400 degrees with the coals lightly covered with ash, add the olive oil into the Dutch oven, followed by the onion, garlic, and sausage pieces. Cook until the onion is brown and the sausage has browned, about 7 minutes. Remove the sausage from the pan and set aside.

3. Next, stir in the pepper flakes, chicken stock, and water and bring to a boil. Cook, uncovered, for about 20 minutes. Add in the kale and boil for about 5 more minutes until tender. Stir in the sausage and cook for about 2 more minutes.

4. Remove the Dutch oven from the grill and season with coarsely ground black pepper and fresh sea salt. Serve hot.

2 tablespoons olive oil

1 medium yellow onion, finely chopped

1 garlic clove, finely chopped

¾ pound homemade pork or chicken sausage, cut into ½-inch pieces

¼ teaspoon red pepper flakes

3 cups homemade Chicken Stock (page 42)

2 cups water

1 pound fresh kale, stemmed and chopped

Coarsely ground black pepper

Fresh sea salt

Sweet Potato Soup with Grilled Bacon and Walnuts

**MAKES 6 SERVINGS • ACTIVE TIME: 45 MINUTES •
TOTAL TIME: 1 HOUR AND 30 MINUTES**

For the most flavor, smoke the bacon and walnuts with maple woodchips. This soup takes a relatively short amount of time to prepare—perfect for a last-minute meal. I recommend serving with a glass of Pinot Grigio or a Sauvignon Blanc.

1. One hour before grilling, soak the maple woodchips in water.

2. Next, place a large Dutch oven on your gas or charcoal grill and prepare to medium heat. Leave the grill covered while heating, as it will add a faint smoky flavor to the skillet.

3. When the grill is ready, at about 400 degrees with the coals lightly covered with ash, throw the woodchips over the coals and cover the grill. When the grill is smoking, add the bacon into the Dutch oven, close the lid, and cook until crispy, about 4 minutes. Meanwhile, place a sheet of aluminum foil on the grill and place the walnuts on it; toast for a couple of minutes. Transfer to a plate covered with paper towels and then break into ½-inch pieces. Set aside.

4. Add the olive oil into the Dutch oven, followed by the shallot and cook for about 5 minutes until translucent. Add in the garlic and cook for another minute until golden.

5. When the garlic is golden, add the sweet potatoes, chicken stock, and water into the pot, and cook for about 15 minutes until the sweet potatoes are easily pierced with a fork.

6. Stir in the ground cinnamon and nutmeg and then remove the Dutch oven from the heat.

7. Using a large food processor or hand-held purée mixer, blend the soup into a desire consistency, and then season with coarsely ground black pepper and fresh sea salt. Finally, top the salad with the bacon bits and serve warm.

TOOLS

2 cups maple woodchips

INGREDIENTS

8 thick slices of bacon, trimmed of excess fat

1 cup walnuts

1 teaspoon olive oil

1 medium shallot, finely chopped

4 garlic cloves, finely chopped

2 to 3 large sweet potatoes, peeled and sliced into thin ½-inch strips

3 cups Chicken Stock (page 42)

1 cup water

⅛ teaspoon ground cinnamon

⅛ teaspoon ground nutmeg

Coarsely ground black pepper

Fresh sea salt

Grilled Split Pea Soup with Ham

MAKES 6 SERVINGS • ACTIVE TIME: 1 HOUR AND 30 MINUTES • TOTAL TIME: 2 HOURS AND 30 MINUTES

Peas fall into the gray area of the Paleo diet, though most dieters chose to eat them. As such, here is my favorite recipe for a split pea soup with ham from my mother, though she will always make it best!

1. Place a large Dutch oven on your gas or charcoal grill and prepare to medium heat. Leave the grill covered while heating, as it will add a faint smoky flavor to the skillet.

2. When the grill is ready, at about 400 degrees with the coals lightly covered with ash, add the olive oil into the Dutch oven, followed by the carrots and yellow onion. Cook for about 5 to 7 minutes until the carrots are tender and the onion is translucent. Stir in the garlic and cook for another minute.

3. Add the split peas, red pepper flakes, and ham into the Dutch oven, and then submerge with the 6 cups of water (you may need more or less depending on the size of the Dutch oven and ham). Cover and cook until the peas have fully cooked into the water, about 1½ to 2 hours. Be sure to restock the grill while cooking.

4. Add the thyme and cook for a few more minutes before removing from grill. Let the soup rest for about 15 minutes so that the soup can thicken, and then season with coarsely ground black pepper and fresh sea salt. Serve hot.

1 tablespoon olive oil

1 cup carrots, chopped into ¼-inch segments

1 medium yellow onion, finely chopped

3 garlic cloves, minced

1 pound dried split peas

¼ teaspoon red pepper flakes

1 ready-to-eat ham, about 4 pounds

6 cups water

2 sprigs thyme, leaves removed

Coarsely ground black pepper

Fresh sea salt

Smoked Manhattan Clam Chowder

MAKES 6 SERVINGS • ACTIVE TIME: 35 MINUTES •
TOTAL TIME: 1 HOUR AND 20 MINUTES

Unlike the non-Paleo version of clam chowder popularized in New England, Manhattan Clam Chowder is tomato based.

1. One hour before grilling, soak the hickory or oak woodchips in water.

2. Next, place a large Dutch oven on your gas or charcoal grill and prepare to medium heat. Leave the grill covered while heating, as it will add a faint smoky flavor to the Dutch oven.

3. When the grill is ready, at about 400 degrees with the coals lightly covered with ash, throw the woodchips over the coals and cover the grill. When the grill is smoking, add the bacon into the Dutch oven, close the lid, and cook until crispy, about 4 minutes. Transfer the bacon onto a plate covered with paper towels and set aside.

4. Add olive oil into the Dutch oven and bring to heat. Next, add in the yellow onion, celery, and green pepper and cook until the onion is translucent and the pepper is tender, about 7 minutes. Stir in the garlic and sear until golden, about a minute.

5. Next, stir in the clam juice and canned tomatoes and cook until the tomatoes have broken down slightly, about 10 to 15 minutes. Stir in the clams, thyme, and parsley, and cook until the clams have opened wide, about 8 minutes. (Some of the clams may not open. In these cases, discard the clams as they will be overcooked and tough.)

6. Remove the Dutch oven from the heat and let rest for 5 minutes. Season with coarsely ground black pepper and fresh sea salt, and serve hot.

VARIATION In season you might prefer to use 3 medium fresh plum tomatoes instead of canned tomatoes. Just add 1 cup of water to the recipe.

TOOLS

2 cups hickory or oak woodchips

INGREDIENTS

4 thick slices of bacon

1 tablespoon olive oil

1 medium yellow onion, finely chopped

3 stalks celery, diced into ¼-inch segments

1 green pepper, stemmed, seeded and diced into ¼-inch segments

2 garlic cloves, minced

1 cup fresh clam juice

20 quahog or cherrystone clams

1 cup canned tomatoes, diced with juice

2 sprigs thyme, leaves removed

1 tablespoon flat-leaf parsley

Coarsely ground black pepper

Fresh sea salt

Smoked Tomato Basil Soup

MAKES 6 SERVINGS • ACTIVE TIME: 2 HOURS • TOTAL TIME: 3 HOURS

This soup is perfect for those cold spring and autumn evenings when you just want to hunker down. As this is a thick soup, I strongly recommend using a Dutch oven over medium heat on the grill. Also, as the smoke will add a strong flavor to the soup, I encourage you to add the woodchips to the coals for only about 15 minutes before the soup is finished, being sure to grill with the lid covered.

TOOLS

Dutch Oven

2 cups hickory or oak woodchips, soaked

INGREDIENTS

¼ cup, plus 3 tablespoons olive oil

2 large yellow onions, finely chopped

5 garlic cloves, finely chopped

2–3 pounds plum tomatoes, seeded and halved

4 cups Chicken Stock (page 42)

3 tablespoons clarified butter

4 cups fresh basil leaves

2 sprigs thyme, leaves removed

Coarsely ground black pepper

Fresh sea salt

1. Place a large Dutch oven on your gas or charcoal grill and prepare to medium heat. Leave the grill covered while heating, as it will add a faint smoky flavor to the Dutch oven.

2. While waiting, add the hickory woodchips into a bowl of water and let soak for at least 1 hour.

3. When the grill is ready, at about 400 degrees with the coals lightly covered with ash, add the 3 tablespoons of olive oil into the Dutch oven, followed by the yellow onion, and then cook for about 5 to 7 minutes. When the yellow onion is lightly brown, stir in the garlic and sear until golden, not brown, about 2 minutes.

4. Next, add the halved tomatoes and the remaining ¼ cup of olive oil. Bring to a simmer and cook for about 5 minutes. Next, mash the tomatoes with a fork and then stir in the chicken stock, clarified butter, basil leaves, and thyme and simmer for about 25 minutes.

5. After about 25 minutes, throw the soaked woodchips onto the coals and cover the grill, letting the tomato basil soup cook for 15 more minutes.

6. Remove the Dutch oven from the grill and let rest for a few minute. If you would like a thinner soup, purée the soup in a food processor until you reach the desired consistency. Season with black pepper and sea salt and serve warm.

Arugula Salad with Tarragon-Shallot Vinaigrette

MAKES 6 SERVINGS • ACTIVE TIME: 10 MINUTES • TOTAL TIME: 15 MINUTES

This hearty salad is quick to make and full of flavor. Serve it with white wine.

1. Rinse the arugula and then dry thoroughly. Place in refrigerator and set aside.

2. In a small bowl, whisk together the shallot, tarragon, lemon juice, and Dijon mustard, and then slowly add in the olive oil and red wine vinegar.

3. Season with coarsely ground black pepper and fresh sea salt, and then pour over the arugula. Serve immediately.

1 pound of Arugula lettuce, stemmed
1 shallot, minced
5 stalks tarragon, minced
¼ small lemon, juiced
1 teaspoon Dijon mustard
½ cup olive oil
3 tablespoons red wine vinegar
Coarsely ground black pepper
Fresh sea salt

Spinach Salad with Red Onion and Maple-Smoked Bacon

MAKES 6 SERVINGS • ACTIVE TIME: 35 MINUTES • TOTAL TIME: 45 MINUTES

This salad is perfect for summer evenings and works well when served with a seafood or poultry dish and some white wine.

1. One hour before grilling, soak the maple woodchips in water.

2. Next, place a large cast-iron skillet on your gas or charcoal grill and prepare to medium heat. Leave the grill covered while heating, as it will add a faint smoky flavor to the skillet.

3. While waiting, rinse the stemmed spinach and dry thorough. Place the spinach in a medium bowl and mix in the red onion and dried cranberries. Transfer to the refrigerator and set aside.

4. When the grill is ready, at about 400 degrees with the coals lightly covered with ash, throw the woodchips over the coals and cover the grill. When the grill is smoking, add the bacon into the cast-iron skillet, close the grill's lid, and cook until crispy, about 4 minutes. Transfer to a plate covered with paper towels and then break into ½-inch pieces. Set aside.

5. In a small bowl, whisk together the balsamic vinegar, Dijon mustard, and red pepper flakes, and then gradually incorporate the olive oil. Season with coarsely ground black pepper and fresh sea salt, and then mix with the spinach salad and bacon bits. Serve chilled.

VARIATION Those who like the heat might want to toss in a couple pepperoncini peppers!

TOOLS

1 cup maple woodchips

INGREDIENTS

1 pound spinach, stemmed

1 medium red onion, sliced into ¼-inch rings

¼ cup dried cranberries

8 thick slices of bacon, trimmed of excess fat

2 tablespoons balsamic vinegar

1 teaspoon Dijon mustard

1 teaspoon red pepper flakes (optional)

½ cup olive oil

Coarsely ground black pepper

Fresh sea salt

Frisée Salad with Maple-Smoked Bacon and Hard-Boiled Eggs

MAKES 6 SERVINGS • ACTIVE TIME: 15 MINUTES • TOTAL TIME: 40 MINUTES

I serve this salad as a main course, sometimes with a side of Grilled Beets with Walnuts (page 281) and typically with a glass of white wine.

1. One hour before grilling, soak the maple woodchips in water.

2. Next, place a large cast-iron skillet on your gas or charcoal grill and prepare to medium heat. Leave the grill covered while heating, as it will add a faint smoky flavor to the skillet.

3. While waiting, rinse the frisée and dry thoroughly. Place the frisée in a medium bowl and store it in the refrigerator.

4. Next, fill a medium saucepan with water and place over medium-heat. Bring to a boil and then add the eggs and remove from heat. Cover the saucepan and let the eggs rest in the hot water for about 10 to 14 minutes. Remove from water and let cool in the refrigerator.

5. When the grill is ready, at about 400 degrees with the coals lightly covered with ash, throw the woodchips over the coals and cover the grill. When the grill is smoking, add the bacon into the cast-iron skillet, close the grill's lid, and cook until crispy, about 4 minutes. Transfer to a plate covered with paper towels and set aside.

6. In a small bowl, whisk together the white wine vinegar, red wine vinegar, Dijon mustard, and olive oil and then set aside.

7. Remove the eggs from the refrigerator and then peel off their shells. Slice the eggs in half and add over the frisée salad. Drizzle the vinaigrette onto the frisée and then top with the bacon bits. Season the eggs with the coarsely ground black pepper and fresh sea salt and then serve the salad immediately.

TOOLS

1 cup maple woodchips

INGREDIENTS

1 pound frisée

3 large eggs

8 thick slices of bacon, trimmed of excess fat

2 tablespoons white wine vinegar

2 tablespoons red wine vinegar

1 teaspoon Dijon mustard

2 tablespoons olive oil

Coarsely ground black pepper

Fresh sea salt

Beet Salad with Toasted Sunflower Seeds over Arugula

MAKES 6 SERVINGS • ACTIVE TIME: 15 MINUTES • TOTAL TIME: 20 MINUTES

1. Rinse the arugula and then dry thoroughly. Set it aside in the refrigerator.

2. Cut the beets into quarters and then combine with ¼ cup olive oil in a small bowl. Let rest for 30 minutes.

3. Place a medium cast-iron skillet on your gas or charcoal grill and prepare it to medium-high heat. Leave the grill covered while heating, as it will add a faint, smoky flavor to the skillet.

4. When the grill is ready, at about 400 to 500 degrees, transfer the beets alone onto the grill (do not place them in the skillet). Grill the beets for about 10 minutes, until tender and marked. Transfer the beets to a large bowl and cover with aluminum foil.

5. Add the sunflower seeds into the cast-iron skillet and cook until browned, about 2 minutes. Remove and mix in with the beets. Set aside.

6. In a small bowl, add the remaining 2 tablespoons of olive oil and balsamic vinegar and mix thoroughly. Drizzle on top of beets and sunflower seeds, and then place over chilled arugula. Season with pepper and salt before serving.

VARIATION Add ½ cup of walnuts when you're toasting the sunflower seeds.

⅓ **pound arugula,
rinsed and stemmed**

6 medium red beets, peeled

¼ **cup plus 2 tablespoons olive oil**

¼ **cup sunflower seeds**

2 tablespoons balsamic vinegar

Coarsely ground black pepper

Fresh sea salt

House Salad

This basic, hearty salad is a good complement to a large steak or pork chop. For something different, pair this with a side of Grilled Scallions (page 263).

3 heads Romaine lettuce

1 small red onion, sliced into ¼-inch rings

10 Kalamata olives

10 green olives

4 plum tomatoes, stemmed and quartered

6 pepperoncini peppers

2 garlic cloves, minced

¼ cup red wine vinegar

¾ cup olive oil

Coarsely ground black pepper

Fresh sea salt

1. Rinse the heads of Romaine lettuce and dry them thoroughly. In a medium bowl, combine the lettuce, red onion, Kalamata olives, green olives, tomatoes, and pepperoncini peppers and then set in refrigerator.

2. In a small jar, whisk together the minced garlic, red wine vinegar, and olive oil, and then season with coarsely ground black pepper and fresh sea salt. Chill in refrigerator for 15 minutes.

3. Remove the salad and the vinaigrette from the refrigerator and mix together. Serve immediately.

Grilled Chicken Tomatillo Soup

MAKES 6 SERVINGS • ACTIVE TIME: 30 MINUTES • TOTAL TIME: 45 MINUTES

This Mexican-inspired soup with some kick is hearty enough to be a main course.

1. Place a large Dutch oven on your gas or charcoal grill and prepare to medium heat. Leave the grill covered while heating, as it will add a faint smoky flavor to the Dutch oven.

2. While waiting for the grill, purée the tomatillos and jalapeño in a food processor with lime juice and set aside.

3. When the grill is ready, at about 400 degrees with the coals lightly covered with ash, heat the olive oil in the Dutch oven. When hot, add the chicken breasts and cook until browned, about 2 to 3 minutes per side. Remove and set aside.

4. Add the white onion and scallions into the Dutch oven and cook until the onion is translucent, about 5 minutes. Stir in the garlic and cook until golden, about 1 minute.

5. Next, add the chicken stock into the Dutch oven, followed by the mixture of tomatillos and jalapeño. Bring to a boil and then reduce heat and simmer for about 15 minutes.

6. On a carving board, slice the chicken into thin strips and add to the soup along with the cilantro. Boil until the chicken is cooked through, about 5 more minutes, and then remove the Dutch oven from the grill. Season with black pepper and sea salt, then serve warm.

VARIATION If you would like a bit more spice, substitute the jalapeño for a habanero pepper.

TOOLS

Food processor

Dutch oven

INGREDIENTS

3 tomatillos, peeled

1 jalapeño, stemmed and semi-seeded

½ small lime, juiced

1 tablespoon olive oil

2 skinless, boneless chicken breasts

1 medium white onion, chopped

3 scallions, finely chopped

2 garlic cloves

4 cups Chicken Stock (page 42)

¼ cup fresh cilantro, finely chopped

Coarsely ground black pepper

Fresh sea salt

Rubs, Marinades & sauces
(Elements of Style)

Apple Cider Marinade

This marinade goes best when used on pork. The apple cider flavor in the pork will go great with some Grilled Tomatoes with Garlic (page 266) and chilled white wine.

2 cups fresh apple cider

¼ cup olive oil

½ lemon, juiced

2 sprigs thyme, leaves removed and finely chopped

2 sprigs rosemary, leaves removed and finely chopped

2 garlic cloves, minced

1 tablespoon coarsely ground black pepper

2 teaspoons fresh sea salt

1. In a medium bowl or roasting pan, combine all the ingredients to the marinade and let rest for 15 minutes for the flavors to spread throughout the marinade.

2. Add your desired meat into the marinade. Transfer to the refrigerator and let marinate from 4 hours to overnight. If the marinade does not fully cover the meat, turn the meat halfway through the marinating process so that all areas of the meat receive equal amounts of the marinade.

Lemon-Salt Rub

Often the simplest flavors are the best. Here, the pairing of the lemon and salt goes perfectly when applied to seafood dishes. When grilling halibut, this is especially my favorite dry rub.

3 tablespoons lemon zest

2 tablespoons coarsely ground black pepper

1 tablespoon fresh sea salt

In a small bowl, thoroughly combine all the ingredients and store at room temperature for up to 1 week.

Ancho Chile Rub

Although you may think that this is a very hot rub, it is fairly mild. Unlike regular chile powder, ancho chile powder comes from the ancho chile pepper, which is actually fairly sweet. As such, I paired the sweet flavors from the ancho chile with the sweet flavor from the paprika.

In a small bowl, mix together all the ingredients and store at room temperature for up to 1 month.

2 tablespoons sweet paprika

1 tablespoon ancho chile powder

1 tablespoon ground coriander

1 tablespoon ground cumin

2 teaspoons dried oregano

1 teaspoon ground allspice

1 teaspoon onion powder

½ teaspoon cinnamon

Classic Seafood Rub

The variety of sweet, natural flavors in this rub is great for seafood, such as a fillet of haddock.

In a small bowl, thoroughly combine all the ingredients and store in an airtight container at room temperature for up to 1 month.

2 tablespoons sweet paprika

2 tablespoons garlic powder

1 tablespoon dry mustard

1 tablespoon ancho chile powder

1 tablespoon onion powder

1 tablespoon coarsely ground black pepper

1 tablespoon fresh sea salt

1 teaspoon ground cinnamon

1 teaspoon ground cumin

Smoked Paprika Rub

This rub is smoky and spicy and has a lot of soul to it. As such, I recommend using this rub with beef, pork, and poultry.

2 tablespoons smoked paprika

2 teaspoons ground coriander

2 teaspoons ground cumin

1 teaspoon cayenne pepper

1 tablespoon coarsely ground black pepper

1 tablespoon fresh sea salt

In a small bowl, thoroughly combine all the ingredients and store at room temperature for up to 1 month.

Smoked Apple-Mustard BBQ Sauce

This sauce goes well with poultry, pork, and lamb dishes and should be generously applied to the meat. Serve with white wine.

1 tablespoon olive oil

¼ small shallot, finely chopped

¼ cup apple cider

¼ cup white wine vinegar

1 tablespoon tequila

2 teaspoons fresh parsley, finely chopped

3 tablespoons fresh fish sauce

1 tablespoon raw honey

1 tablespoon Dijon mustard

2 teaspoons hot Chinese mustard

Coarsely ground black pepper

Fresh sea salt

Combine all the ingredients into a small bowl and refrigerate for 1 hour before applying to the meat. This sauce is perfect used for ribs and applied to meats before grilling.

Paprika-Onion Rub

The rich flavors of sweet paprika are often compared to a red bell pepper without the heat, and because of that, it pairs well with minced onion and garlic. This is a great rub for beef, lamb, and poultry.

In a small bowl, thoroughly combine all the ingredients and store at room temperature for up to 5 days.

½ white onion, minced

4 garlic cloves, minced

¼ cup sweet paprika

2 teaspoons ground cumin

1 teaspoon cayenne pepper

1 teaspoon fresh thyme

1 teaspoon fresh oregano

1 teaspoon coarsely ground black pepper

1 teaspoon fresh sea salt

Lime-Curry Rub

Great when used on a rack of lamb or a whole grilled chicken, this rub has a soft, mild flavoring that goes great with larger cuts of meat.

Using your hands, thoroughly mix the ingredients to the rub in a small bowl, kneading gently to eliminate any clumps that form in the rub. Store in an airtight container at room temperature for up to 1 week.

½ medium lime, juiced

1 tablespoon fresh cilantro

1 tablespoon yellow curry powder

1 tablespoon coarsely ground black pepper

2 teaspoons fresh sea salt

Memphis Rub

This very strong rub is perfect when you are grilling up some beef or pork ribs. Knead it firmly into the meaty parts of the ribs so that the meat is filled with succulent flavor.

2 tablespoons coarsely ground black pepper

1 tablespoon smoked paprika

2 teaspoons yellow mustard seeds

2 teaspoons fresh sea salt

1 teaspoon ground cumin

1 teaspoon dried oregano

1 teaspoon garlic powder

½ teaspoon cayenne pepper

In a small bowl, thoroughly combine all the ingredients and store in an air-tight container at room temperature for up to 1 month.

Lemon-Rosemary Marinade

This is a delicious marinade for poultry. The tart flavor of the lemon complements the soft, natural flavors of the rosemary, and their result is wonderful. If using this marinade on a whole grilled chicken or turkey, take a handful of additional rosemary sprigs and the used lemon halves, and add to the bird's cavity. Tie away with some butcher's string.

4 lemons, halved

6 garlic cloves

3 sprigs fresh thyme, leaves removed

3 sprigs fresh rosemary, leaves removed

2 teaspoons ground fennel

1 tablespoon organic honey

1 tablespoon coarsely ground black pepper

1 tablespoon fresh sea salt

1. In a medium bowl or roasting pan, combine all the ingredients to the marinade and let rest for 15 minutes for the flavors to spread throughout the marinade.

2. Add your desired meat into the marinade. Transfer to the refrigerator and let marinate from 4 hours to overnight. If the marinade does not fully cover the meat, turn the meat halfway through the marinating process so that all areas of the meat receive equal amounts of the marinade.

Balsamic Marinade

The balsamic marinade should be used primarily on smaller cuts of beef such as the fillet, beef kebabs, or a hangar steak.

1. In a medium bowl or roasting pan, combine all the ingredients to the marinade and let rest for 15 minutes for the flavors to spread throughout the marinade.

2. Add your desired meat into the marinade. Transfer to the refrigerator and let marinate from 4 hours to overnight. If the marinade does not fully cover the meat, turn the meat halfway through the marinating process so that all areas of the meat receive equal amounts of the marinade.

4 sprigs fresh basil

2 sprigs fresh rosemary, leaves removed

2 garlic cloves, crushed

2 teaspoons Dijon mustard

1 teaspoon raw honey

1 cup olive oil

¼ cup balsamic vinegar

1 tablespoon coarsely ground black pepper

1 tablespoon fresh sea salt

Mint Marinade

In general, mint is most often paired with lamb. However, I find that it is also great when used on poultry with Beefsteak Tomatoes and Basil (page 35).

1. In a medium bowl or roasting pan, combine all the ingredients to the marinade and let rest for 15 minutes for the flavors to spread throughout the marinade.

2. Add your desired meat into the marinade. Transfer to the refrigerator and let marinate from 4 hours to overnight. If the marinade does not fully cover the meat, turn the meat halfway through the marinating process so that all areas of the meat receive equal amounts of the marinade.

½ cup olive oil

½ cup fresh mint leaves, finely chopped

¼ cup dry red wine

4 garlic cloves, finely chopped

1 tablespoon fresh parsley, finely chopped

1 tablespoon coarsely ground black pepper

2 teaspoons fresh sea salt

Indian Curry Rub

This rub should be used primarily on poultry and lamb. Grilled Cubanelle Peppers and Plum Tomatoes (page 262) are a great side to accompany the flavors from this rub.

2 tablespoons yellow curry powder
1 tablespoon smoked paprika
1 tablespoon ground ginger
2 teaspoons ground cumin
2 teaspoons ground allspice
2 teaspoons coarsely ground black pepper
1 teaspoon fresh sea salt

In a small bowl, thoroughly combine all the ingredients to the rub and store in an airtight container at room temperature for up to 1 month.

Indian Chile Rub

For a Sunday with the boys, this is such a great rub to use for chicken wings and thighs. Toss a little olive oil with the wings and thighs and then smoke them on the grill with some hickory or oak woodchips. Consider adding some fresh chopped parsley into the rub as it will complement the curry flavoring.

3 tablespoons ancho chile powder
1 tablespoon red pepper flakes
1 tablespoon ground turmeric
1 tablespoon ground coriander
1 tablespoon ground fennel
1 tablespoon ground cumin
1 tablespoon coarsely ground black pepper
2 teaspoons fresh sea salt
1 teaspoon ground cloves

In a small bowl, thoroughly combine all the ingredients to the rub and store in an airtight container at room temperature for up to 1 month.

Oregano-Garlic Rub

Oregano and garlic are complementary flavors that go great on pork and poultry. This rub is best when prepared fresh since the flavor of the fresh oregano lessens as it is stored for longer periods of time.

In a small bowl, thoroughly combine all the ingredients to the rub and store in an airtight container at room temperature for up to 1 week.

1 tablespoon fresh oregano, finely chopped

2 garlic cloves, minced

2 sprigs thyme, leaves removed

2 teaspoons coarsely ground black pepper

1 teaspoon fresh sea salt

1 teaspoon ground cumin

1 teaspoon ground coriander

Toasted Fennel Seed Rub

This recipe requires you to toast the fennel and coriander seeds before grinding into a rub. Toasting these seeds brings out their natural flavor, while also adding a rustic flavor to the rub. This recipe is best when used on poultry and seafood.

1. Place a small frying pan over medium heat and toast the fennel and coriander seeds, about 1 to 2 minutes. Remove from heat and let cool.

2. When cool, place the seeds in a small, sealable plastic bag. Using the dull side of the knife, press and grind both the fennel and coriander seeds, as well as the whole black peppercorns, into a rub, and then stir in the fresh sea salt.

¼ cup fennel seeds

1 tablespoon coriander seeds

2 teaspoons whole black peppercorns

2 teaspoons fresh sea salt

Lemon-Parsley Marinade

Use this marinade for quick, last-minute meals, especially seafood dishes, as both the lemon and parsley flavors are mild when grilled. Pair with white wine.

2 medium lemons, juiced

2 garlic cloves, finely chopped

¼ cup fresh parsley, finely chopped

¼ cup fresh basil, finely chopped

1 tablespoon red bell pepper, finely chopped

1 tablespoon coarsely ground black pepper

2 teaspoons fresh sea salt

½ cup olive oil

1. In a medium bowl or roasting pan, combine all the ingredients to the marinade and let rest for 15 minutes for the flavors to spread throughout the marinade.

2. Add your desired meat into the marinade. Transfer to the refrigerator and let marinate from 4 hours to overnight. If the marinade does not fully cover the meat, turn the meat halfway through the marinating process so that all areas of the meat receive equal amounts of the marinade.

Mango Marinade

This is the perfect marinade to use when grilling swordfish. Serve with a side of Grilled Asparagus (page 256) or Grilled Eggplant (page 272).

1 ripe mango, peeled, pitted and chopped

2 tablespoons olive oil

¼ medium orange, juiced

2 teaspoons fresh ginger, finely chopped

2 teaspoons organic honey

2 garlic cloves, finely chopped

2 teaspoons coarsely ground black pepper

2 teaspoons fresh sea salt

½ teaspoon cayenne pepper

1. In a medium bowl or roasting pan, combine all the ingredients to the marinade and let rest for 15 minutes for the flavors to spread throughout the marinade.

2. Add your desired meat into the marinade. Transfer to the refrigerator and let marinate from 4 hours to overnight. If the marinade does not fully cover the meat, turn the meat halfway through the marinating process so that all areas of the meat receive equal amounts of the marinade.

Mojo Marinade

The Mojo marinade always goes well with pork, poultry, and seafood. The fresher the ingredients and the longer you marinate the meat with the Mojo Marinade the better.

1. In a medium bowl or roasting pan, combine all the ingredients to the marinade and let rest for 15 minutes for the flavors to spread throughout the marinade.

2. Add your desired meat into the marinade. Transfer to the refrigerator and let marinate from 4 hours to overnight. If the marinade does not fully cover the meat, turn the meat halfway through the marinating process so that all areas of the meat receive equal amounts of the marinade.

4 to 6 oranges, juiced (about 1½ cups)

3 medium limes, juiced

1 medium lemon, juiced

½ cup fresh oregano, finely chopped

6 garlic cloves, finely chopped

1 jalapeño, seeded and finely chopped

½ cup olive oil

1 tablespoon coarsely ground black pepper

2 teaspoons fresh sea salt

Maple BBQ Sauce

The maple flavor that comes from the maple syrup works so well with all pork recipes. Try this as a basting sauce for some pork ribs.

1. Place a medium saucepan over medium-high heat. When hot, add in the onion and garlic cook until the onion is translucent and the garlic is golden, not brown, about 1 to 2 minutes.

2. Add in the remaining ingredients and bring to a boil.

3. Reduce the sauce to a simmer and the cook, uncovered, for about 20 minutes.

4. When the sauce has reduced to about 1 to 2 cups, remove from heat and refrigerate for an hour before serving.

¼ small white onion, finely chopped

2 garlic cloves, minced

1 cup Paleo Ketchup (page 77)

3 tablespoons apple cider vinegar

1 tablespoon clarified butter

½ cup organic maple syrup

2 tablespoons organic molasses

2 teaspoons ground mustard

Coarsely ground black pepper

Fresh sea salt

White Wine Marinade

This is a classic marinade that always goes well with poultry and seafood. Because it is such a classic recipe, it is used as a foundational recipe to most marinades. I encourage you to add and subtract to this recipe so that you can find the best fit for flavors.

¼ cup dry white wine

¼ cup olive oil

2 tablespoons fresh parsley, finely chopped

2 tablespoons fresh oregano, finely chopped

1 medium lemon, juiced

1 medium shallot, finely chopped

2 garlic cloves, finely chopped

1 teaspoon Dijon mustard

2 teaspoons coarsely ground black pepper

2 teaspoons fresh sea salt

1. In a medium bowl or roasting pan, combine all the ingredients to the marinade and let rest for 15 minutes for the flavors to spread throughout the marinade.

2. Add your desired meat into the marinade. Transfer to the refrigerator and let marinate from 4 hours to overnight. If the marinade does not fully cover the meat, turn the meat halfway through the marinating process so that all areas of the meat receive equal amounts of the marinade.

Cilantro Lime Marinade

Cilantro is one of my favorite herbs, and I love it on or alongside nearly every cut of meat. As such, I cannot limit this marinade to only one or two categories of meat, but rather encourage you to try it on everything. Serve with Jalapeños Filled with Sausage and Diced Tomatoes (page 28).

2 limes, juiced

¼ cup olive oil

¼ cup fresh cilantro, finely chopped

2 garlic cloves, finely chopped

2 teaspoons coarsely ground black pepper

2 teaspoons fresh sea salt

½ teaspoon organic honey

1. In a medium bowl or roasting pan, combine all the ingredients to the marinade and let rest for 15 minutes for the flavors to spread throughout the marinade.

2. Add your desired meat into the marinade. Transfer to the refrigerator and let marinate from 4 hours to overnight. If the marinade does not fully cover the meat, turn the meat halfway through the marinating process so that all areas of the meat receive equal amounts of the marinade.

Paleo Ketchup

One of the simplest yet most compatible and fundamental sauces, Paleo Ketchup goes great as a foundation to nearly all BBQ sauces. And, of course, everyone needs Paleo Ketchup.

1. In a medium bowl, combine the tomato paste, lemon juice, raw honey, ground mustard, onion powder, ground cloves, and all spice.

2. Gradually whisk in the water, and serve. For a more flavorful ketchup, store the ketchup in the refrigerator overnight.

¾ cup tomato paste
¼ medium lemon, juiced
1 tablespoon raw honey
¼ teaspoon ground mustard
¼ teaspoon onion powder
1/8 teaspoon ground cloves
1/8 teaspoon all spice
½ cup water

Hot & Spicy Chile Rub

Consider yourself warned, this is not for those who are timid of spice. Because of the intensity of the heat, I love using this rub on smaller sections of meat so that it is not overpowering. Try this with hangar steak, chicken breasts, and pork chops.

In a small bowl, thoroughly combine all the ingredients and store in an airtight container at room temperature for up to 1 month.

3 tablespoons chile powder
3 tablespoons smoked paprika
1 tablespoon dried oregano
2 teaspoons ground cumin
2 teaspoons coarsely ground black pepper
2 teaspoons fresh sea salt
1 teaspoon dried thyme

Smoked Southern BBQ Sauce

This sauce is filled with intense spice and goes great when served on or alongside barbecued beef and pork dishes. The habanero pepper is optional in this recipe and should be used only for those who like their BBQ sauces hot!

TOOLS

2 to 3 cups hickory or oak woodchips

INGREDIENTS

2 garlic cloves, finely chopped

1 medium white onion, finely chopped

1½ cups canned crushed tomatoes

½ cup tomato paste

¼ cup white wine vinegar

¼ cup balsamic vinegar

2 tablespoons Dijon mustard

1 medium lime, juiced

2 tablespoons ginger, finely chopped

1 teaspoon smoked paprika

½ teaspoon ground cinnamon

2 dried chipotle peppers, finely chopped

1 habanero pepper, seeded and finely chopped (optional)

1 cup water

Coarsely ground black pepper

Fresh sea salt

1. An hour before grilling, add the woodchips into a bowl of water and let soak.

2. Prepare your gas or charcoal grill to medium-high heat.

3. While waiting for the grill to heat up, place a small frying pan over medium heat and, when hot, add the garlic and onion and cook until the garlic has browned and the onion is translucent. Remove and set aside.

4. Transfer the cooked garlic and onion into a food processor, followed by the tomatoes and tomato paste. Puree into a thick paste, and then add the remaining ingredients to the food processor and blend thorough. Transfer the sauce into to a medium saucepan and set alongside the grill.

5. When the grill is ready, about 400 to 450 degrees with the coals lightly covered with ash, drain 1 cup of the woodchips and spread over the coals or pour in the smoker box. Place the medium saucepan on the grill and then bring the sauce to a boil with the grill's lid covered, aligning the air vent away from the woodchips so that their smoke rolls around the sauce before escaping. Let the sauce cook for about 30 to 45 minutes, every 20 minutes adding another cup of drained woodchips, until it has reduced to about 2 cups.

6. Remove the sauce from the heat and serve warm. The sauce can be kept refrigerated for up to 2 weeks.

Beef

Perhaps no other type of meat is associated with a Paleo diet more so than beef. After all, beef is our go-to meat when it comes to flame and coal—and what's more primal than that?

This past summer my son John and I explored grilling over a straight-up wood fire using a small handmade Mexican clay fire pit. Initially, this was more an act of luck than anything else!

We had come home with two beautifully hand-cut 1½-inch porterhouse steaks when we realized we had overlooked a critical component to our big dinner—a grill! We had just moved into our newly renovated home, a 1755 farmhouse along the coast of Maine, and our Weber gas and charcoal grills were both out of commission. We did have plenty of aged firewood and I suddenly remembered that before the renovations we had moved a clay fire pit to the edge of the yard. With a bit of scraping and brushing from a few available broken branches (that later became our kindling), we got this little clay cooking pit up and running. Now we just needed a grill to cover the open face of our cooking contraption. And we were in luck: Though our kettle charcoal grill was not ready, the stainless steel grill grate was just large enough to cover the entire mouth of the clay fire pit. We were in business!

As we stoked the fire and watched a nice bed of coals take shape, we added three split and well-seasoned 16-inch slabs of wood across the flame, and the fire rose higher. John seasoned the porterhouses with fresh-cracked black peppercorns and fresh sea salt. With our Weber kettle, we usually wait for white coals to accumulate at the bottom before we put the beef on the girl. But this combination—a shallow bed of coals and fresh raw flame from newly added timbers—looked ready to do the job. Five minutes on each side was all it took.

Our contractor had recently given us a beautiful gift: a cutting block made from the reclaimed timbers of a 200-year-old barn. The two succulent porterhouses, seared with lovely black lines, were a vision of beauty on the deep-golden wood.

There is an art to grilling: a fine balance between the cut of meat, the temperature of flame, the quality of the smoke, and just the right amount of time for these influences to work their magic. When that balance is just so—well, dinner is served! And those por-

terhouses, standing entirely on their own, were perfection. What might have been an utter disaster, with a bit of ingenuity and a fair amount of luck, allowed us to dine like kings.

As great as those two steaks were, the best part was sharing the experience with my son. Food is a celebration of life—from the animal that was raised, to the time we spend planning, seasoning, and patiently working flame and temperature. And who better to celebrate with than the ones you love?

We hope the recipes that follow will guide the way as you create feasts to remember. Enjoy!

—John F. Whalen Jr.

New York Strip

**MAKES 2 TO 3 SERVINGS • ACTIVE TIME: 15 MINUTES •
TOTAL TIME: 1 HOUR AND 30 MINUTES**

For my family, this is our go-to steak. Grilling the New York Strip can be quick or long, depending on your timing. Letting the steak rest at room temperature for an hour is not necessary, so if you are in a rush please feel free to skip it. However, if you do have the time, definitely let the steaks absorb the oil so that they are grizzled and tender when pulled from the grill.

1. Remove the steaks from the refrigerator and rub with the olive oil and let rest at room temperature for 1 hour.

2. A half hour before cooking, prepare your gas or charcoal grill to medium-high heat.

3. When the grill is ready, about 400 to 450 degrees with the coals lightly covered with ash, season one side of the steaks with half of the coarsely ground pepper and sea salt.

4. Place the seasoned-sides of the steaks on the grill at medium heat. Wait 3 to 5 minutes until they are slightly charred. One minute before flipping, season the uncooked sides of the steaks with the remaining pepper and sea salt. Turn the steaks and grill for another 3 to 4 minutes for medium-rare, and 4 to 5 minutes for medium. The steaks should feel slightly firm if poked in the center.

5. Remove the steaks from the grill and transfer to a large cutting board. Let stand for 10 minutes, allowing the steaks to properly store their juices and flavor. Serve warm, and if desired, garnish with a little rosemary.

**2 New York strip steaks,
about 1½ inches thick**

2 tablespoons olive oil

Coarsely ground black pepper

Fresh sea salt

Rosemary for garnish, if desired

TIP: FOR MORE OF A NATURAL FLAVOR, LIGHT A FIRE USING DRY LOGS AND BURN DOWN TO COALS. THIS WILL TAKE THE GRILL ABOUT 45 MINUTES TO PREHEAT, AND THE STEAKS WILL NEED TO COOK FOR ABOUT ONE MINUTE LONGER THAN DESIRED TEMPERATURE ON EACH SIDE.

Rib Eye

Rib Eye

MAKES 2 TO 3 SERVINGS • ACTIVE TIME: 15 MINUTES •
TOTAL TIME: 1 HOUR AND 30 MINUTES

A classic Rib Eye is my favorite cut of meat. When you go to your local butcher, take the extra time to find organically raised and grass-fed meat, as the flavors will explode in your mouth. The Rib Eye is best when well marbled, so be sure to request this from your butcher. Always get a thick steak, and consider serving this steak with some Grilled Shishito Peppers (page 260).

1. Rub both sides of the steaks with olive oil and let rest at room temperature for about 1 hour.

2. A half hour before cooking, prepare your gas or charcoal grill to medium-high heat.

3. When the grill is ready, about 400 to 450 degrees with the coals lightly covered with ash, season one side of the steaks with half of the coarsely ground pepper and sea salt. Place the seasoned-sides of the steaks on the grill and cook for about 6 to 7 minutes until blood begins to rise from the tops. Season the tops of the steaks while waiting. When the steaks are charred, flip and cook for 4 to 5 more minutes for medium-rare and 5 to 6 more minutes for medium. The steaks should feel slightly firm if poked in the center. (I recommend cooking the rib eye to medium; medium-rare will be very chewy and tough. For a boneless rib eye, cook for 2 to 4 minutes less.)

4. Remove the steaks from the grill and transfer to a large cutting board. Let stand for 5 to 10 minutes, allowing the steaks to properly store their juices and flavor. Serve warm.

2 bone-in rib eyes, about 1¼ to 1½ inches thick

2 tablespoons olive oil

Coarsely ground black pepper

Fresh sea salt

TIP: THE RIB EYE IS OFTEN BARBEQUED WITH RUBS AND MARINADES, THOUGH I TEND TO FIND IT BEST WHEN SERVED WITH CILANTRO OIL (PAGE 197).

Porterhouse

This is by far one of the most filling and flavorful steaks available—it boasts half New York Strip and half Filet Mignon. Ask your butcher to keep a large part of the filet mignon intact (they sometimes trim it too much).

2 porterhouse steaks, about 1½ inches thick

4 tablespoons olive oil

Coarsely ground black pepper

Fresh sea salt

Rosemary, if desired as garnish

TIP: FOR A BIT OF A SAN FRANCISCO FLARE, MIX THE OLIVE OIL WITH A COUPLE TEASPOONS OF FINELY CHOPPED GARLIC BEFORE MARINATING THE STEAKS.

1. Rub both sides of the steaks with olive oil and let rest at room temperature for about 1 hour.

2. A half hour before cooking, prepare your gas or charcoal grill to medium-high heat.

3. When the grill is ready, about 400 to 450 degrees with the coals lightly covered with ash, season one side of the steaks with half of the coarsely ground pepper and sea salt. Place the seasoned-sides of the steaks on the grill and cook for about 5 to 6 minutes, seasoning the tops of the steaks while waiting. When the steaks are charred, flip and cook for 4 to 5 more minutes for medium-rare, and 6 to 7 for medium. The steaks should feel slightly firm if poked in the center.

4. Remove the steaks from the grill and transfer to a large cutting board. Let stand for 10 minutes, allowing the steaks to properly store their juices and flavor. Serve warm.

let Mignon

filet is one of the harder steaks to grill due to its 2-inch thickness and
...tively small surface area, proving it difficult to remain upright on the
...te. As such, I recommend using a seasoned cast-iron skillet over the
...ll for the initial searing and then transferring the filets to the oven.

Tie the butcher's string tightly around each steak. Then rub
...h sides of the steaks with the 2 tablespoons olive oil and
...rest at room temperature for about 1 hour.

A half hour before cooking, place the cast-iron skillet on
... grate and prepare your gas or charcoal grill to medium-
...h heat. Leave the grill covered while heating, as it will add
...int, smoky flavor to the skillet.

When the coals are ready, about 400 degrees with the coals
...htly covered with ash, season one side of the steaks with
...lf of the coarsely ground pepper and sea salt.

Spread the remaining tablespoon of olive oil in the
...llet, and then place the steaks, seasoned sides down, into
...e cast iron skillet. Wait 2 to 3 minutes until they are slightly
...arred, seasoning the uncooked sides of the steaks with the
...naining pepper and sea salt while waiting. Turn the steaks
...d sear for another 2 to 3 minutes. Remove from the skillet
...d let rest, uncovered, for 30 minutes.

Preheat the oven to 400 degrees.

Put the steaks back into the cast-iron skillet and place in
...e oven. For medium-rare, cook for 11 to 13 minutes,
...d for medium, cook for 14 to 15.

Remove the steaks from the oven and transfer to a large
...tting board. Let stand for 10 minutes. Remove the butcher's
...ing from the steaks and serve warm.

**2 filet mignon steaks,
about 2 to 2½ inches thick**

3 tablespoons olive oil

Coarsely ground black pepper

Fresh sea salt

1 to 2 feet of butcher's string

TIP: WHEN YOU REMOVE THE
STEAKS FROM THE GRILL, DO
NOT RELINQUISH THE FIRE, AS
IT COULD STILL BE USED TO
GRILL CUBANELLE (PAGE 262)
OR SHISHITO PEPPERS
(PAGE 260).

Basic Flank Steak

**MAKES 2 SERVINGS • ACTIVE TIME: 15 MINUTES •
TOTAL TIME: 1 HOUR AND 15 MINUTES**

ie flank steak, often hailed as a chewy cut of meat, is one of the hardest
cook properly. Stay close to the grill after you put the steaks on as it is very
sy for them to be overcooked. Also, because the steak is very thin, be sure
prepare the grill to medium-high heat so that the edges will be charred
d crisp.

Remove the steak and rub with a mixture of the olive oil,
emary, and thyme. Let rest at room temperature for 1 hour.

A half hour before cooking, prepare your gas or charcoal
ll to medium-high heat.

When the grill is ready, about 400 to 450 degrees with the
ls lightly covered with ash, season one side of the steak
h half of the coarsely ground pepper and sea salt.
ce the seasoned side of the steak on the grill and cook
about 4 to 5 minutes, seasoning the uncooked side of the
ak while waiting. When the steak seems charred, gently
and cook for 4 to 5 more minutes for medium-rare and
ore minutes for medium. The steak should feel slightly
n if poked in the center.

Remove the steak from the grill and transfer to a large
ting board. Let stand for 6 to 8 minutes. Slice the steak
gonally into long, thin slices. Serve warm.

1 flank steak, about 1 to 1½ pounds

2 tablespoons olive oil

2 sprigs of rosemary,
leaves removed

2 sprigs of thyme, leaves removes

Coarsely ground black pepper

Fresh sea salt

TIP: DUE TO THE FLANK'S
TOUGHNESS, IT IS ESSENTIAL
TO SLICE THIS STEAK INTO
VERY THIN STRIPS.

Balsamic Glazed Flank Steak with Vidalia Onions & Mushrooms

**MAKES 2 TO 3 SERVINGS • ACTIVE TIME: 30 MINUTES •
TOTAL TIME: 1 HOUR AND 45 MINUTES**

Because of the balsamic glaze, the flank becomes much more tender than usual. I recommend serving with the Vidalia onions and mushrooms since the balsamic pairs nicely with them.

Rub the steak with olive oil and let rest at room temperature for about 1 hour.

A half hour before cooking, prepare your gas or charcoal grill to medium-high heat.

While waiting, heat olive oil in a wide skillet over low heat. Add the onion slices and mushrooms and sear, stirring frequently, for 15 to 20 minutes until the onions are translucent and tender.

When the grill is ready, about 400° to 450° and the coals are lightly covered with ash, season one side of the steak with half of the coarsely ground pepper and sea salt. Place the seasoned side of the steak on the grill and cook for about 4 to 5 minutes, seasoning the uncooked side of the steak while waiting. When the steak seems charred, gently flip and cook for 4 to 5 more minutes for medium-rare and 6 more minutes for medium. The steak should feel slightly firm if poked in the center.

Remove the steak from the grill and transfer to a large cutting board. Let stand for 6 to 8 minutes.

Add the balsamic vinegar to a small saucepan and bring to a boil over high-heat. Reduce to about ½ cup, about 6 to 7 minutes, and then stir in the clarified butter and rosemary. Remove from heat and season with pepper and salt.

Slice the steak diagonally into long, thin slices. Serve warm with the onions and mushrooms, and drizzle the balsamic glaze on top.

STEAK INGREDIENTS

1 flank steak, about 1 to 1½ pounds

2 tablespoons olive oil

Coarsely ground black pepper

Fresh sea salt

GLAZE INGREDIENTS

1 cup balsamic vinegar

2 tablespoons clarified butter

1 sprig rosemary, leaves removed

Coarsely ground black pepper

Fresh sea salt

VIDALIA ONIONS & MUSHROOMS INGREDIENTS

1½ pounds Vidalia onions, sliced to about ½ inch

1 pound mushrooms of your choice

2 tablespoons olive oil

TIP: ALWAYS CUT FLANK STEAK INTO VERY THIN STRIPS.

Bistecca Alla Fiorentina

Bistecca Alla Fiorentina

MAKES 2 SERVINGS • ACTIVE TIME: 30 MINUTES • TOTAL TIME: 1 HOUR AND 45 MINUTES

Cooked to medium-rare, these steaks will stand by themselves. There is no real need for a side—maybe just a thin slice of lemon—but if you really want one, I suggest Grilled Tomatoes with Garlic (page 262).

I first had this steak when I was sixteen, traveling with my family in Florence, Italy. We had been walking the streets for nearly two hours looking for a place to eat. It was 5:00 on New Year's Eve and everything was booked. Finally, we came across a small storefront with fresh cuts of meat hanging in the window and a man leaning against the door. We asked him if he had room for five. He looked at his watch and asked us if we could eat in under 40 minutes. We told him we would and quickly ordered four Bisteccas Alla Fiorentina with grilled tomatoes with thyme and olive oil. The steaks came out 15 minutes later, still sizzling with the oil shining in the candlelight.

Remove the steaks and place in a roasting pan or bowl. Then, rub the steaks with the rosemary, garlic, and ½ cup olive oil, and let rest at room temperature for 1 hour.

A half hour before cooking, prepare your gas or charcoal grill to medium-high heat.

When the grill is ready, about 400 to 450 degrees with the coals lightly covered with ash, season one side of the steak with half of the coarsely ground pepper and sea salt. Place the seasoned side of the steak on the grill and cook for 5 minutes, basting the unseasoned sides with the remaining olive oil every 30 seconds. Season the top sides with the remaining salt and pepper and then gently flip and cook for 4 to 6 more minutes, still basting until finished. The steak should feel slightly firm if poked in the center.

Remove the steaks from the grill and transfer to a large cutting board. Let stand for 6 to 8 minutes. Serve warm.

2 T-bone steaks, about ¾ to 1¼ inches thick

4 cloves garlic, crushed

1 cup olive oil

1 sprig of rosemary, leaves removed

Coarsely ground black pepper

Fresh sea salt

Steak au Poivre

MAKES 2 TO 3 SERVINGS • ACTIVE TIME: 25 MINUTES •
TOTAL TIME: 1 HOUR AND 15 MINUTES

This is a classic style that is often paired with a T-bone or porterhouse. However, because of its rich flavor and powerful spice, I recommend applying it to the New York Strip or Filet Mignon. If doing the Filet, follow the recipe on page 93, using the cast-iron skillet and following the given cooking times.

Rub both sides of the steaks with olive oil and let rest at
om temperature for about 1 hour.

A half hour before cooking, prepare your gas or charcoal
ll to medium-high heat.

Seal the peppercorns in a small, sealable plastic bag and
ush with the bottom of a cast-iron skillet.

When the grill is ready, at about 400 to 450 degrees with
e coals lightly covered with ash, press the peppercorns and
salt firmly into both sides of the steak. Place the seasoned
es of the steaks on the grill at medium heat and cook for 4
5 minutes until they are slightly charred. Turn the steaks
d grill for another 3 to 4 minutes for medium-rare, and 4 to
inutes for medium. The steaks should feel slightly firm if
ced in the center.

Remove the steaks from the grill and transfer to a large
ting board. Let rest for 10 minutes, allowing the steaks to
perly store their juices and flavor.

While the steaks rest, heat the clarified butter in a small
cepan over medium heat. Add the minced shallot, stirring
asionally until softened, about 1 to 2 minutes.

Carefully add the Cognac, and if it flames, shake the pan and
it for the flame to burn out. Boil until it has reduced by half.

Next, mix in the coconut milk until the sauce has slightly
ckened, about 2 to 3 minutes, and then add the parsley
l salt.

Place the steaks onto warmed plates and spoon the sauce
top of the steaks.

STEAK INGREDIENTS

**2 New York strip steaks,
about 1½ inches thick**

2 tablespoons olive oil

6 tablespoons black peppercorns

Fresh sea salt

SAUCE INGREDIENTS

3 tablespoons clarified butter

1 shallot, minced

½ cup Cognac

½ cup coconut milk

**2 tablespoons parsley,
finely chopped**

Fresh sea salt

Porterhouse with Chimichurri Sauce

MAKES 2 TO 3 SERVINGS • ACTIVE TIME: 35 MINUTES • TOTAL TIME: 2 HOURS

The Argentinian Chimichurri sauce goes well with any steak. It can be used as marinade, though this is sometimes a little risky because of the light kick from the Fresno chile. I suggest serving the chimichurri sauce on the side, and for those who would like even more heat in the sauce, substitute a habanero in place for the Fresno chile!

Rub both sides of the steaks with olive oil and let rest at
[r]om temperature for about 1 hour.

A half hour before cooking, prepare your gas or charcoal
[gr]ill to medium-high heat.

While you wait, combine the vinegar, garlic, shallot, scal-
[li]on, Fresno chile, lemon juice, and salt in a medium bowl and
[le]t rest for 15 minutes. Next, add the parsley, cilantro, and
[or]egano, then gradually whisk in the olive oil. Set aside.

When the grill is ready, at about 400 to 450 degrees with
[th]e coals lightly covered with ash, season one side of the
[st]eaks with half of the coarsely ground pepper and sea salt,
[as] well as a very light brush of the sauce along the bone.

Place the seasoned-sides of the steaks on the grill and cook
[fo]r about 5 to 6 minutes, seasoning the tops of the steaks
[w]hile waiting. Again, lightly trace the bone with the sauce.
[W]hen the steaks are charred, flip and cook for 4 to 5 more
[m]inutes for medium-rare, and 6 to 7 for medium. The steaks
[sh]ould feel slightly firm if poked in the center.

Remove the steaks from the grill and transfer to a large
[cu]tting board. Let stand for 10 minutes, allowing the steaks
[to] properly store their juices and flavor. Serve warm with the
[c]himichurri sauce on the side.

STEAK INGREDIENTS

2 Porterhouse steaks,
about 1½ inches thick

4 tablespoons olive oil

Coarsely ground black pepper

Fresh sea salt

SAUCE INGREDIENTS

½ cup red wine vinegar

4 garlic cloves, minced

1 shallot, minced

½ scallion, minced

1 Fresno chile, finely chopped
(for additional spice, substitute
for a minced habanero)

1 tablespoon fresh lemon juice

1 teaspoon fresh sea salt

½ cup flat-leaf parsley, minced

½ cup cilantro, minced

2 tablespoons, minced oregano

¾ cup olive oil

Chipotle Rib Eye

**MAKES 2 TO 3 SERVINGS • ACTIVE TIME: 20 MINUTES •
TOTAL TIME: 1 HOUR AND 30 MINUTES**

This is a spiced dish that is not for those who dislike flavor. Serve with a glass of red wine.

Combine the rub ingredients and mix thoroughly.

Rub a very thin layer of olive oil to both sides of the steaks and then generously apply the dry rub, firmly pressing it all around the steak. Let rest at room temperature for at least 1 hour.

A half hour before cooking, prepare your gas or charcoal grill to medium-high heat.

When the grill is ready, at about 400 to 450 degrees with the coals lightly covered with ash, place the steaks on the grill and cook for about 6 to 7 minutes until blood begins to rise from the tops. When the steaks are charred, flip and cook for 4 to 5 more minutes for medium-rare and 5 to 6 more minutes for medium. The steaks should feel slightly firm if poked in the center.

Remove the steaks from the grill and transfer to a large cutting board. Let stand for 5 to 10 minutes, allowing the steaks to properly store their juices and flavor. Serve warm.

STEAK INGREDIENTS

2 bone-in rib eyes, about 1¼ to 1½ inches thick

1 tablespoon olive oil

RUB INGREDIENTS

2 dry chipotle peppers, seeded and finely minced

1 tablespoon dried oregano

1 tablespoon dried cilantro

1 tablespoon coarsely ground black pepper

2 teaspoons ground cumin

1 teaspoon onion powder

½ teaspoon dry mustard

Fresh sea salt

Chile-Rubbed London Broil

**MAKES 2 TO 3 SERVINGS • ACTIVE TIME: 30 MINUTES •
TOTAL TIME: 1 HOUR AND 30 MINUTES**

he London broil is an economical steak for large family gatherings.
tart with a tasty rub, and finish by slicing the London broil
iagonally into thin strips.

Combine the rub ingredients and mix thoroughly. Set aside.

Rub a very thin layer of olive oil to both sides of the steaks
nd then generously apply the dry rub, firmly pressing it all
ound the steak. Let rest at room temperature for at least
hour.

A half hour before cooking, prepare your gas or charcoal
ill to medium-high heat.

When the grill is ready, at about 400 to 450 degrees with
e coals lightly covered with ash, place the steaks on the
ill. Cook for until blood begins to rise from the tops, about 4
5 minutes. When the steaks are charred, flip and cook
r another 3 to 4 minutes for medium-rare, and 5 to 6 for
edium.

Remove the steak from the grill and transfer to a large
utting board. Let stand for 6 to 8 minutes. Slice the steak
iagonally into long, thin slices. Serve warm.

STEAK INGREDIENTS

1 London broil steak,
about ¾ to 1 inch thick

1 to 2 tablespoons olive oil

RUB INGREDIENTS

1 cup ancho chile powder

2 tablespoons paprika

1 tablespoon coarsely
ground black pepper

1 tablespoon sea salt

2 teaspoons cumin

1 teaspoon cayenne pepper

1 teaspoon dry mustard

1 teaspoon oregano

TIP: DUE TO THE LONDON
BROIL'S TOUGHNESS,
IT NEEDS TO BE SLICED
INTO VERY THIN STRIPS.

Butcher's Steak

MAKES 2 SERVINGS • **ACTIVE TIME: 15 MINUTES** •
TOTAL TIME: 1 HOUR AND 30 MINUTES

I first heard of this steak in a review of the restaurant St. Anselm in Brooklyn, New York. Aside from the tremendous reviews, I went to this restaurant because my father and brother both attended St. Anselm College in Manchester, New Hampshire. The Butcher Steak, or the Hanger Steak, is such a phenomenal piece of meat when cooked properly. Be sure to marinate this dish in oil beforehand so that the steak is charred and gristly after grilling.

STEAK INGREDIENTS

2 hanger steaks, about
1 to ½ pounds each

Coarsely ground black pepper

Fresh sea salt

MARINADE INGREDIENTS

3 cups olive oil

6 cloves garlic, crushed

3 sprigs of rosemary

3 sprigs thyme

¼ lemon, juiced

1. Combine the ingredients of the marinade in a small, rectangular dish. Lay the steaks into the dish so that the marinade completely covers the steaks. If not, add more olive oil until it does. Cover with aluminum foil and place in the refrigerator and let rest for at least 4 hours.

2. Remove the steaks from the refrigerator and let stand at room temperature for about 1 hour.

3. A half hour before cooking, prepare your gas or charcoal grill to medium-high heat.

4. When the grill is ready, at about 400 to 450 degrees with the coals lightly covered with ash, remove the steaks from the marinade and season with the coarsely ground pepper and sea salt. Set the marinade aside.

5. Place the seasoned-side of the steak on the grill. Cook for about 4 to 5 minutes, basting the steaks with the remaining marinade every 30 seconds. When the steak is charred, gently flip and cook for 3 to 4 more minutes for medium-rare, and 5 for medium. The steaks should feel slightly firm if poked in the center.

6. Remove the steaks from the grill and transfer to a large cutting board. Let stand for 5 to 10 minutes, allowing the steaks to properly store their juices and flavor. Serve warm.

Skirt Steak with Olive Tapenade

MAKES 2 TO 3 SERVINGS • ACTIVE TIME: 30 MINUTES • TOTAL TIME: 1 HOUR AND 50 MINUTES

The skirt steak is often referred to as the chewiest piece of meat. However, because of how thin it is, it is very easy to overcook the steak, which then promotes the chewiness. As such, grill these steaks over direct heat and make sure not to cook past medium.

Rub both sides of the steaks with olive oil and let rest at room temperature for about 1 hour.

While waiting, combine the tapenade ingredients in a medium bowl and mix thoroughly. Set aside.

A half hour before cooking, prepare your gas or charcoal grill to extremely high heat.

When the grill is ready, about 500 to 600 degrees with the coals lightly covered with ash, season the steaks with the coarsely ground pepper and sea salt. Place the steaks on the grill and spoon the tapenade onto the top of each steak. Cook for about 3 minutes and then flip. Again, add the tapenade and cook for about 2 to 3 minutes for medium-rare, and 3 to 4 for medium. The steaks should be very charred and slightly firm cooked in the center.

Remove the steaks from the grill and transfer to a large cutting board. Let stand for 5 to 10 minutes. Slice the steak diagonally into long, thin slices and arrange the tapenade on the side. Serve warm. The tri-tip should be slightly firm and when instant-read thermometer is inserted into the roast's thickest section, it should read around 125 degrees.

STEAK INGREDIENTS

2 skirt steaks, about 1 to 1 ½ pounds each and ½ to ¾ inch thick

2 tablespoons olive oil

Coarsely ground black pepper

Fresh sea salt

TAPENADE INGREDIENTS

1 cup Niçoise olives, pitted and chopped

½ cup olive oil

½ small shallot, minced

1 garlic clove, minced

1 sprig of rosemary, leaves removed and finely minced

1 anchovy fillet (optional)

1 tablespoon basil, finely chopped

1 tablespoon flat-leaf parsley, finely chopped

1 tablespoon capers, minced

1 tablespoon thyme

1 teaspoon red pepper flakes

Red Wine & Herbs Marinated Tri-Tip Steak

MAKES 3 SERVINGS • ACTIVE TIME: 45 MINUTES • TOTAL TIME: 14 HOURS

he Tri-Tip is great for large gatherings in the summer. I love grilling
iis out on the patio on the Fourth of July and then enjoying it just before
ie fireworks. Serve with Grilled Balsamic Peppers (page 265).

The day before grilling, combine the ingredients for
arinade in a large sealable plastic bag and let rest at room
mperature. After 20 minutes, add the tri-tip roast to the
g so that it is completely submerged; more wine may
necessary. Seal and place in refrigerator and let
irinate overnight.

One hour before grilling, remove the tri-tip bag from
e refrigerator and let stand at room temperature.

Prepare your gas or charcoal grill, designating 2 sections:
e for direct medium-high heat and the other for indirect
it.

When the grill is ready, at about 400 to 450 degrees with
coals lightly covered with ash, remove the roast from
marinade and grill over direct heat for about 5 minutes
side. Next, move the roast to the indirect heat and cover
grill. Cook for another 20 to 30 minutes, flipping
ry 5 minutes.

Remove the steaks from the grill and transfer to a large
ting board. Let stand for 10 minutes, allowing the steaks
properly store their juices and flavor, and then slice across
grain into thin slices. Serve warm.

STEAK INGREDIENTS

1 tri-tip roast, about 1½ inches
thick and 2 to 2½ pounds

MARINADE INGREDIENTS

2 cups red wine

2 tablespoons red wine vinegar

2 garlic cloves, crushed

2 sprigs of rosemary,
leaves removed and minced

2 sprigs of thyme, leaves
removed and minced

½ small white onion, finely chopped

1 teaspoon fresh lemon juice

½ teaspoon dried oregano

Coarsely ground black pepper

Fresh sea salt

TIP: IT IS IMPORTANT TO
NOTE THAT THIS STEAK
REQUIRES MARINATING OVER-
NIGHT SO THAT IT SOFTENS
AND BECOMES MORE TENDER
ON THE GRILL.

Filet Mignon with Red Wine Reduction

MAKES 2 TO 3 SERVINGS • ACTIVE TIME: 30 MINUTES • TOTAL TIME: 2 HOURS

A red wine reduction is perfect when accompanying the filet mignon. Prepare the reduction in the cast-iron skillet after it has been used for the filet; this simple choice will bring out the most in the flavor in the reduction.

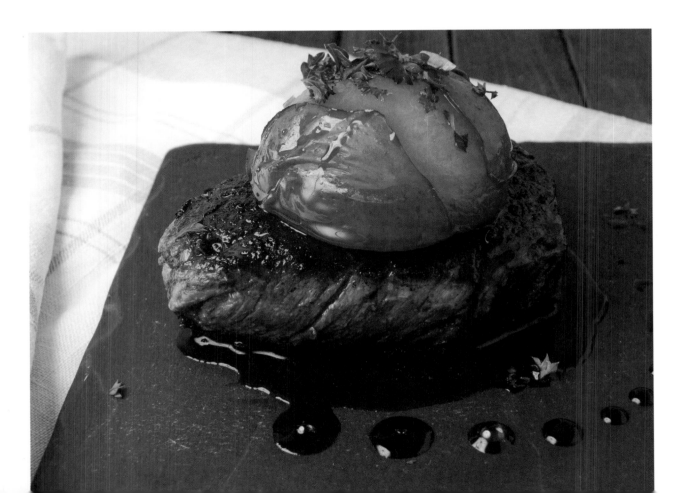

Tie the butcher's string tightly around each steak. Then, rub both sides of the steaks with 2 tablespoons of olive oil and let rest at room temperature for about 1 hour.

A half hour before cooking, place the cast-iron skillet on the grate and prepare your gas or charcoal grill to medium-high heat. Leave the grill covered while heating, as it will add a faint, smoky flavor to the skillet.

When the grill is ready, at about 400 degrees with the coals lightly covered with ash, season one side of the steaks with half of the coarsely ground pepper and sea salt.

Spread the remaining tablespoon of olive oil in the skillet, and then place the steaks, seasoned sides down, into the skillet. Wait 2 to 3 minutes until they are slightly charred, seasoning the uncooked sides of the steaks with the remaining pepper and sea salt while waiting. Turn the steaks and sear for another 2 to 3 minutes. Remove from filets from the skillet and let rest, uncovered, for 30 minutes. Leave the skillet on the grill.

Preheat the oven to 400 degrees.

While waiting for the oven, add the coconut oil to the skillet and wait 30 seconds, scrapping the browned bits left by the filets from the bottom of the skillet. Stir in the shallots, garlic, and oregano and sauté for about 2 minutes until tender and lightly browned. Add the Port, dry white wine, and balsamic vinegar and simmer until thickened and reduced by half. Add the parsley and simmer for 1 minute. Remove the skillet from heat and pour the reduction into a small bowl. Season with pepper and salt. Cover with aluminum foil and set aside.

Place the filets back into the cast-iron skillet and transfer to oven. For medium-rare, cook for 11 to 13 minutes, and for medium, cook for 14 to 15.

Remove the steaks from the oven and transfer to a large cutting board. Let stand for 10 minutes. Cut loose the butcher's string. Spoon the sauce over the filets and serve warm.

STEAK INGREDIENTS

2 filet mignon steaks, about 2 to 2½ inches thick

1 to 2 feet of butcher's string

3 tablespoons olive oil

Coarsely ground black pepper

Fresh sea salt

SAUCE INGREDIENTS

2 tablespoon coconut oil

½ shallot, finely chopped

1 tablespoon garlic, minced

1 teaspoon fresh oregano, finely chopped

1 cup Port wine

1 cup dry white wine

3 tablespoons balsamic vinegar

¼ cup fresh parsley, finely chopped

Coarsely ground black pepper

Fresh sea salt

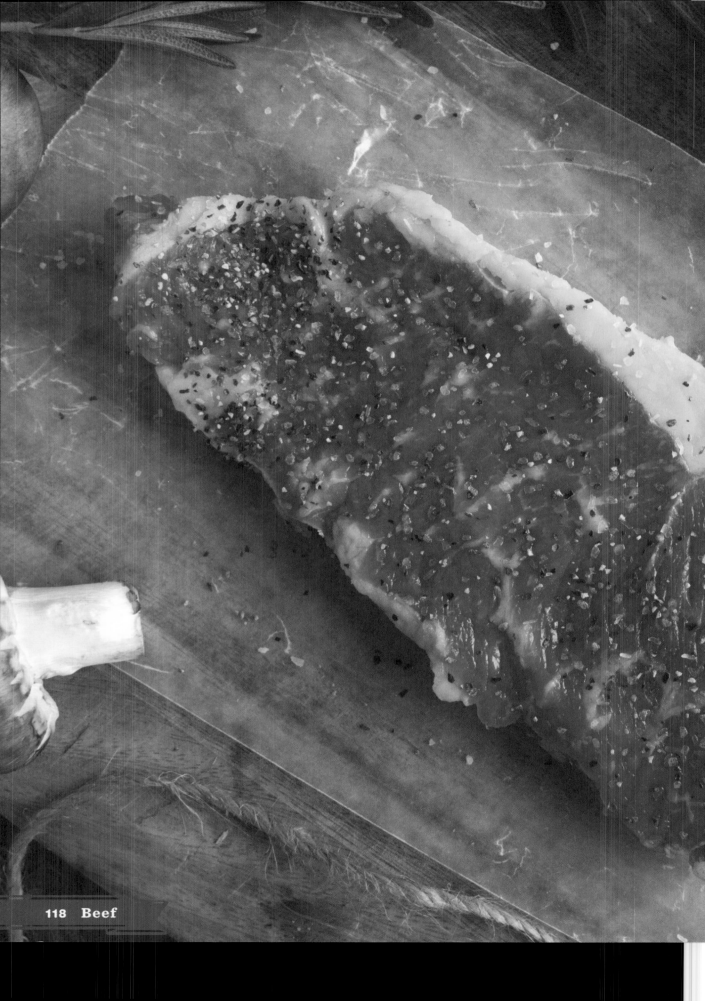

New York Strip with Pizzaiola Sauce

New York Strip with Pizzaiola Sauce

**MAKES 2 TO 3 SERVINGS • ACTIVE TIME: 35 MINUTES •
TOTAL TIME: 1 HOUR AND 50 MINUTES**

I first had a version of this dish at The Palm Restaurant in New York City. My father and I ordered two New York Strips and then, rather unexpectedly, we ordered a side of green beans and marinara. Combine the steak, green beans, and pizzaiola (slightly more complex than a classic marinara) into one bite, and the flavors will make this dish one of your favorites. You can always grill the green beans, too, using a cast-iron skillet.

Remove the steaks from the refrigerator and rub with
tablespoons of olive oil. Let rest at room temperature
or 1 hour.

A half hour before cooking, place the cast-iron skillet on
he grate and prepare your gas or charcoal grill to medium-
igh heat. Leave the grill covered while heating, as it will add
faint, smoky flavor to the skillet.

When the grill is ready, at about 400 degrees with the coals
ghtly covered with ash, season one side of the steaks with
alf of the coarsely ground pepper and sea salt.

Spread the remaining tablespoon of olive oil in the
killet, and then place the steaks, seasoned sides down,
ito the cast-iron skillet. Wait 2 to 3 minutes until they are
lightly charred, seasoning the uncooked sides of the steaks
vith the remaining pepper and sea salt while waiting. Turn
he steaks and sear for another 2 to 3 minutes. Remove from
llets from the skillet and let rest, uncovered, for 30 minutes.
eave the skillet on the grill.

Preheat the oven to 400 degrees.

While waiting for the oven, add the olive oil into the
killet, scraping the brown bits off the bottom of the pan.
Vhen the oil is hot, add the garlic and cook until golden, about
0 seconds to 1 minute. Add the plum tomatoes, sun-dried
omatoes, oregano, rosemary, thyme, and red pepper flakes.
immer for 15 minutes. Add the wine and basil and season
ith pepper and salt. Simmer for 20 more minutes, then re-
love the skillet from the grill and cover with aluminum foil.

Your oven should be preheated. Transfer the strips onto a
oasting pan and place in the oven. Cook for 6 to 8 minutes for
edium-rare, and 10 to 12 for medium.

Remove the steaks and transfer to a large cutting board
nd let stand for 10 minutes. Place the steaks on warm
eds of pizzaiola.

STEAK INGREDIENTS

**2 New York strip steaks,
about 1½ inches thick**

3 tablespoons olive oil

Coarsely ground black pepper

Fresh sea salt

SAUCE INGREDIENTS

¼ cup olive oil

4 garlic cloves, finely chopped

**2 pounds plum tomatoes,
crushed by hand**

¼ cup sun-dried tomatoes

1 sprig oregano

1 sprig rosemary

1 sprig thyme

**1 teaspoon red pepper
flakes (optional)**

¼ cup dry white wine

½ cup basil, finely chopped

Coarsely ground black pepper

Fresh sea salt

TIP: FOR A REALLY RICH
PIZZAIOLA, FIRST USE A CAST-
IRON SKILLET FOR THE SEARING
OF THE STEAKS, AND THEN USE
IT FOR COOKING THE SAUCE.

Blackened Texas Brisket with Coleslaw

**MAKES 3 TO 4 SERVINGS • ACTIVE TIME: 8 TO 9 HOURS •
TOTAL TIME: 10 TO 11 HOURS**

Beef brisket is a cut from the chest muscles and is known for its toughness
when cooked over high-heat. To tenderize the meat, we must grill the brisket
at low-heat, 225 to 250 degrees, for a long period of time, about 5 to 7 hours.
When cooked properly, the brisket will be tender and juicy. Coleslaw is the
perfect accompaniment.

Combine the rub ingredients in a small bowl and whisk thoroughly. Rub the brisket with the olive oil and then generously apply the rub ingredients, firmly kneading it into the meat. Wrap the brisket in plastic wrap and let rest at room temperature from 2 to 10 hours (the longer the better).

While waiting, soak the woodchips in water for to 2 hours.

A half hour before cooking, prepare your gas or charcoal grill to low heat: about 250 degrees. You want to designate two separate heat sections on the grill: one for direct-heat and the other for indirect-heat. To do this, simply arrange the coals toward one side of the grill.

When the grill is ready (the coals should be lightly covered with ash), drain 1 cup of the woodchips and spread over the coals or pour in the smoker box. Place the grate on the grill and then lay the brisket, fatty-side up, in the large aluminum pan. Position the pan over the cool section of the grill and then cover with the lid, aligning the air vent away from the woodchips so that their smoke rolls around the brisket before escaping. Cook for 5½ to 6 hours, rekindling the fire with coals and fresh wood chips every hour or so. When the internal temperature reads 190 to 200 degrees, and the meat is very tender when pierced with a fork, remove from the grill.

Transfer to a large cutting board and let stand for 20 to 30 minutes without touching.

While waiting, put a saucepan over medium-low heat and add all of the ingredients for the coleslaw except for the cabbage and carrots. Bring to a boil and simmer for 5 minutes. Add the cabbage and carrots to a medium-sized bowl. Remove the dressing from heat and slowly stir into the cabbage and carrots. Refrigerate for 30 minutes.

Slice the brisket diagonally into ½-inch strips and serve with coleslaw.

TOOLS

6 to 8 cups hickory or oak woodchips

1 large, aluminum foil pan

1 smoker box (if using gas grill)

STEAK INGREDIENTS

1 center-cut beef brisket, 5 to 6 pounds and about ½ inches thick

2 tablespoons olive oil

RUB INGREDIENTS

¼ cup of paprika

3 tablespoons coarsely ground black pepper

1 tablespoon ground chipotle chile

1 tablespoon chili powder

2 teaspoons cayenne pepper

1 teaspoon ground cumin

1 teaspoon dried oregano

Fresh sea salt

COLESLAW INGREDIENTS

¼ cup apple cider vinegar

¼ cup raw honey

1 garlic clove, minced

1 teaspoon celery salt

1 teaspoon coarsely ground black pepper

1 teaspoon fresh sea salt

½ teaspoon dry mustard

½ head purple cabbage

½ head green cabbage

2 carrots, peeled and finely chopped

Paleo Hamburger with Sun-Dried Tomato Pesto and Portobello Mushrooms

Paleo Hamburger with Sun-Dried Tomato Pesto and Portobello Mushrooms

MAKES 4 TO 5 SERVINGS • ACTIVE TIME: 1 HOUR AND 15 MINUTES • TOTAL TIME: 2 HOURS AND 15 MINUTES

This specialty hamburger takes a little while to make—from the baking of the buns to the grilling of the Portobello Mushrooms. But it's so worth it.

HAMBURGER INGREDIENTS

1 pound ground sirloin

1 pound ground chuck

½ small shallot, finely chopped

Coarsely ground black pepper

Fresh sea salt

1 head romaine lettuce

2 tomatoes, sliced at ¼ inch

1 red onion, sliced at ¼ inch

HAMBURGER BUN INGREDIENTS

¾ cup cashews

2 large eggs

1 teaspoon apple cider vinegar

1 teaspoon baking powder

¼ cup coconut flour

¼ cup almond flour

3 tablespoons ghee

1 teaspoon fresh sea salt

½ cup water

1 teaspoon sesame seeds

1. Mix with your hands the sirloin, chuck, and shallot in a large bowl. With your hands, form the meat into patties about 1¼ to 1½ inches thick and season with the salt and pepper. To prevent the burgers from rising on the grill, take your thumb and make a small divot in the center of each patty.

2. Rub the Portobello mushrooms with the 4 tablespoons of oil and let rest, with the hamburgers, at room temperature for 1 hour.

3. Preheat your oven to 350 degrees.

4. In a small food processor, pulse the cashews to a flour. Slowly add the rest of the ingredients besides the sesame seeds, and then blend into a dough. Remove from processor and form the dough into medium-sized buns, placing them onto a baking ban. Sprinkle the sesame seeds on top. Transfer to oven and cook for about 20 to 25 minutes until golden brown. Remove and let cool.

. A half hour before cooking, prepare your gas or charcoal grill to medium-high heat.

. In a small food processor, combine the pesto ingredients except for the olive oil and pulse into a thick mixture. Slowly add the olive oil and process until reaching the consistency of your liking. Set aside.

. Place the burgers and the mushrooms on the grill and cook for 3 to 4 minutes each side. Brush the mushrooms with the remaining olive oil each minute. Transfer to a plate and let rest for 3 to 5 minutes.

. Serve burgers warm on buns with lettuce, tomato, and red onion. Place the Portobello on top of each hamburger, and then top with a scoop of pesto.

PORTOBELLO MUSHROOM INGREDIENTS

4 to 6 large Portobello mushrooms, stems removed

6 tablespoons olive oil

PESTO INGREDIENTS

1 cup basil leaves

½ cups sun-dried tomatoes

¼ small shallot, finely chopped

¼ cup pine nuts

1 garlic clove, minced

1 tablespoon coarsely ground black pepper

1 teaspoon fresh sea salt

½ cup olive oil

Grilled Beef Short Ribs with Red Wine & Basil Marinade

MAKES 4 TO 5 SERVINGS • ACTIVE TIME: 1 HOUR • TOTAL TIME: 8 HOURS

Beef Short Ribs are extremely soft and delicate after marinating. You can eat these with your hands, but set the table with forks and knives for the bits that fall off the bone.

1. The night before you plan on grilling, combine all the ingredients for the marinade except for the wine in a large bowl or roasting pan. Add the short ribs and pour in the wine. Move the bowl to the refrigerator and let rest for 4 to 6 hours.

2. Transfer the ribs from the marinade to a large cutting board or plate and let stand at room temperature for 1 hour. Season one side of the ribs with half of the pepper and salt.

3. A half hour before cooking, prepare your gas or charcoal grill to medium-high heat.

4. When the grill is ready, at about 400 to 450 degrees with the coals lightly covered with ash, place the seasoned sides of the ribs on the grill and cook for about 4 minutes. Season the tops of the ribs while waiting. When the steaks are charred, flip and cook for 4 more minutes.

5. Transfer the ribs to a cutting board and let rest for 5 to 10 minutes. Serve warm.

SHORT RIB INGREDIENTS

3 to 4 pounds beef short ribs, meaty and cut into 3 to 5 inches

Coarsely ground black pepper

Fresh sea salt

RED WINE & BASIL MARINADE INGREDIENTS

2 cups basil leaves, finely chopped

2 large carrots, finely chopped

2 large onions, finely chopped

2 garlic cloves, finely chopped

1 scallion, finely chopped

2 sprigs thyme, leaves removed

2 sprigs rosemary, leaves removed

2 sprigs oregano, leaves removed

3 tablespoons olive oil

1 bottle dry red wine

Grilled Meatballs in Marinara Sauce

**MAKES 4 SERVINGS • ACTIVE TIME: 1 HOUR •
TOTAL TIME: 1 HOUR AND 35 MINUTES**

Who doesn't love homemade meatballs
in a traditional marinara sauce?

1. In a large bowl, combine with your hands the beef, veal, and onion, and then slowly add in the almond flour. Let rest for 5 minutes and then add in the rest of the ingredients. Let stand at room temperature for 30 minutes.

2. A half hour before cooking, place a cast-iron skillet on your gas or charcoal grill and prepare the grill to medium-high heat. Leave covered while heating, as it will add a faint, smoky flavor to the skillet.

3. Using your hands, firmly form the meat into balls 1½ to 2 inches wide. Place on a plate and set alongside grill.

4. When the grill is ready, at about 400 degrees and lightly covered with ash, add the 2 tablespoons of olive oil into the skillet. When hot, add the meatballs one by one and sear on all sides for about 8 minutes, or until all sides are browned. Remove from skillet and set aside.

5. Next, add the remaining ¼ cup of olive oil to the skillet, scraping off brown bits from the bottom. When the oil is hot, add the garlic and cook until golden, about 30 seconds to 1 minute: Do not let brown. Add the tomatoes, oregano, rosemary, thyme, and the seared meatballs. Simmer for 15 minutes. Add the wine, basil, pepper, and salt and simmer for 20 more minutes, until the meatballs are cooked through.

6. Remove the cast-iron skillet from the grill and spoon the meatballs and sauce into warmed bowls.

MEATBALL INGREDIENTS

1 pound ground beef

1 pound ground veal

1 large yellow onion, finely chopped

¼ cup almond flour

3 garlic cloves, minced

2 large eggs, beaten

¼ cup tablespoons flat-leaf parsley, minced

2 tablespoons basil leaves, minced

1 tablespoon red pepper flakes

Fresh sea salt

MARINARA INGREDIENTS

¼ cup olive oil, plus 2 tablespoons

4 garlic cloves, minced

2 pounds plum tomatoes, crushed by hand

1 sprig oregano

1 sprig rosemary

1 sprig thyme

¼ cup dry white wine

½ cup basil, finely chopped

1 teaspoon coarsely ground black pepper

1 teaspoon fresh sea salt

TIP: FOR A SPICY KICK, STIR SOME GRILLED SHISHITO PEPPERS (PAGE 260) INTO THE SAUCE JUST BEFORE SERVING.

Marinated Steak Kebabs with Salsa Verde and Grilled Cherry Tomatoes

MAKES 3 TO 4 SERVINGS • ACTIVE TIME: 45 MINUTES • TOTAL TIME: 4 HOURS

Everyone loves steak on a stick! The Salsa Verde can be refrigerated overnight and served alongside basically anything, though it really complements these kebabs.

1. Cut the top sirloin into 1½- to 2-inch cubes. Combine the olive oil, basil leaves, rosemary, and garlic in a large sealable bag, then add the cuts of meat. Seal tight and let rest at room temperature for 2 to 3 hours.

2. A half hour before cooking, prepare your gas or charcoal grill to medium-high heat.

3. When the sirloin cuts have finished marinating, remove from bag and take 3 to 4 pieces of meat and pierce with the skewers. At the same time, drizzle the olive oil over the tomatoes in a bowl and sprinkle with thyme. Season with black pepper. Set aside.

4. In a small food processor, add the parsley, cilantro, shallot, anchovy, capers, garlic cloves, and red wine vinegar. Pulse into a thick paste. Remove from processor and place into a small bowl. Whisk in the olive oil and set aside.

5. When the grill is ready, at about 400 degrees with the coals lightly covered with ash, place the kebabs on the grill. Grill the kebabs for about 8 to 9 minutes for medium-rare, 10 minutes for medium. Rotate the kebabs about every 2 minutes so each side is cooked evenly. After 4 minutes, add the oiled tomatoes and cook until the skin is a little crispy and blistered.

6. Remove kebabs and tomatoes from grill and transfer to a large cutting board. Let rest for five minutes and then serve warm with the tomatoes and Salsa Verde.

KEBAB INGREDIENTS

2 to 3 pounds top sirloin

1 cup olive oil

¼ cup basil leaves

1 sprig rosemary, leaves removed

1 garlic clove, minced

SALSA VERDE INGREDIENTS

1 cup Italian parsley leaves

½ cup cilantro

¼ very small shallot

1 anchovy fillet

1 tablespoon capers

2 garlic cloves

1 teaspoon red wine vinegar

½ cup olive oil

TOMATO INGREDIENTS

3 tablespoons olive oil

8 to 12 cherry tomatoes, still on vine

1 sprig thyme, leaves removed

Coarsely ground black pepper

Prime Rib Roast

MAKES 6 TO 7 SERVINGS • ACTIVE TIME: 1 HOUR AND 30 MINUTES • TOTAL TIME: 4 TO 5 HOURS

This dish comes from my mother who will spend the entire day of Christmas preparing this meal so that is just right. The Prime Rib Roast is a very simple dish to make, and as you prepare it more and more, you learn how to perfect it. Serve this on a special occasion with a glass of red wine.

1. Rub the rib roast with olive oil and let rest at room temperature for 30 minutes.

2. Season the rib roast generously using half of the pepper and salt listed. Let rest for another 30 minutes.

3. Prepare your gas or charcoal grill to medium-high heat.

4. When the grill is ready, at about 400 to 450 degrees with the coals lightly covered with ash, place the rib roast in the middle of the grill and sear each side, including the ends, for about 2 to 3 minutes each.

5. Transfer the rib roast from the grill to a large cutting board and let sit for about 30 minutes.

6. Position a large roasting rack and pan in the middle of your oven and preheat to 350 degrees. You want the roasting rack to be very hot so that its grates will instantly sear the rib roast when you place it in.

7. On the cutting board, finely chop the leaves from 1 bunch of the thyme and rosemary and mix with the remaining pepper and salt. Take the rib roast and roll over the mixture so the entire roast is thinly coated. Mix the minced garlic cloves with the ½ teaspoon of olive oil so that it forms a paste. Rub the rib roast lightly with the paste.

8. Divide the remaining 2 bunches of thyme and rosemary evenly, and tuck into the creases between the ribs.

9. Place the rib roast fatty side up onto the roasting pan and cook for the following times:
- Rare: 15 minutes per pound
- Medium-rare: 20 minutes per pound

10. Take the roast out of the oven when a meat thermometer reads 120 degrees. Transfer to a large carving board and let stand for 10 to 15 minutes before carving. Serve with asparagus and cherry tomatoes for a festive-looking meal.

RIB ROAST INGREDIENTS

Rib roast (1 rib will feed 1 to 2 people)

2 tablespoons coarse sea salt

2 tablespoons coarsely ground black pepper

4 garlic cloves, minced

½ teaspoon of olive oil

3 bunches fresh thyme

3 bunches fresh rosemary

TIP: WHEN COOKING A RIB ROAST, ALWAYS REMOVE FROM OVEN ABOUT 5 DEGREES BEFORE DESIRED TEMPERATURE. WHEN YOU REMOVE THE RIB ROAST AND TRANSFER TO A CUTTING BOARD, IT WILL STILL CONTINUE TO COOK FOR ABOUT 10 MORE MINUTES AND WILL RAISE THE INTERNAL TEMPERATURE ABOUT 5 DEGREES.

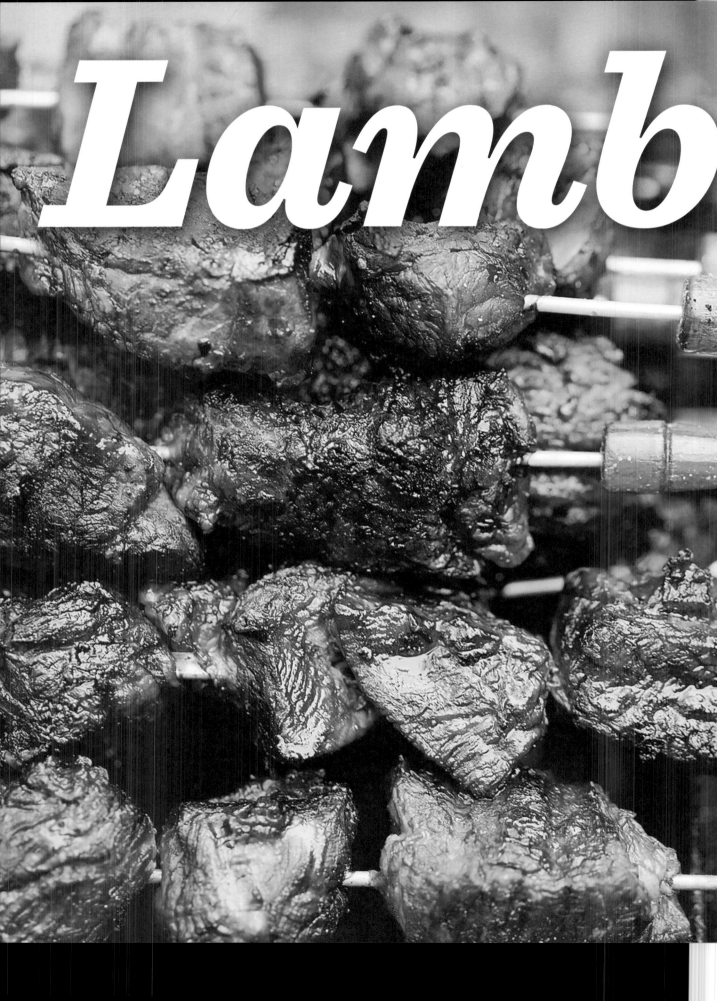

Lamb

Less than 1 percent of the meat eaten in the United States is lamb, while New Zealanders consume about 57 pounds of lamb per person a year, and Greek cuisine is simply unimaginable without lamb. In the United States, it's not so much because we don't like it, but rather because we just are not used to it.

Lamb recipes typically go in one of two directions: with light flavors like mint, rosemary, and lemon in European dishes (like Lamb Chops with Parsley-Mint Sauce, page 147), or with more peppery and smoky flavors from cumin, cinnamon, or turmeric in Middle Eastern dishes (like Lamb Meatballs in Spicy Tomato Sauce, page 156). We've got both types covered. But we also have a simple salt-pepper-and-oil rub (Grilled Lamb Chops, page 141), and because lamb is so flavorful, you don't necessarily need anything more.

Much of that flavor comes from fat, of course. A handful of butchers recommend leaving the fat on the meat so that it really seeps into it and allows it to be more tender. However, when a meat is too fatty, it will serve as a blanket over random parts of the meat, causing uneven temperatures across the cut. Likewise, when grilling lamb, we strongly recommend that you trim the fat from the edges but leave it be wherever it is marbled further into the cut. If you see it fit, you can always add soaked hickory or oak woodchips to the grill toward the end if you crave that smoky flavor.

Grilled Lamb Chops

**MAKES 4 SERVINGS • ACTIVE TIME: 15 MINUTES •
TOTAL TIME: 1 HOUR AND 30 MINUTES**

The grilled lamb chop is a happy median between the classic pork chop and New York strip. Lamb is a very tender meat, so when you season with coarsely ground black pepper and fresh sea salt, lean toward the lighter side so that you don't overdo it. My favorite sauce to go along the lamb chop is Cilantro Oil (page 197).

1. Rub the lamb chops with the olive oil and let rest at room temperature for 1 hour.

2. A half hour before grilling, prepare your gas or charcoal grill to medium-high heat.

3. When the grill is ready, about 400 to 450 degrees, with the coals lightly covered with ash, season one side of the chops with coarsely ground pepper and sea salt.

4. Place the seasoned sides of the chops on the grill at medium heat. Wait 3 minutes until they are slightly charred. One minute before flipping, season the uncooked sides of the chops with the remaining pepper and sea salt. Turn the chops and grill for another 3 minutes for medium-rare, and about 4 minutes for medium. The chops should feel slightly firm if poked in the center.

5. Remove the lamb chops from the grill and transfer to a large cutting board. Let stand for 10 minutes, allowing the lamb to properly store its juices and flavor. Serve warm.

4 lamb chops, about 1¼ inches thick

2 tablespoons olive oil

Coarsely ground black pepper

Fresh sea salt

Rosemary and Lemon Oiled Leg of Lamb

MAKES 4 SERVINGS • ACTIVE TIME: 45 MINUTES • TOTAL TIME: 14 HOURS

As the rosemary and lemon flavors are relatively soft, they go perfectly when used in a marinade for a leg of lamb.

1. The day before you plan to grill, combine the olive oil, rosemary leaves, lemon juice, and garlic in a roasting pan and mix thoroughly.

2. Place the leg of lamb on a large carving board. Season generously with coarsely ground black pepper and sea salt, kneading the lamb so that the pepper and salt are pressed in. Place the seasoned leg of lamb in the roasting pan.

3. Transfer the pan to the refrigerator and let the meat marinate overnight. Note that the olive oil may not cover the meat entirely; in that case, flip the meat once every halfway through the marinating process.

4. An hour before grilling, remove the leg of lamb from the refrigerator and let stand at room temperature for at least 1 hour. Reserve the remaining marinade as it will be used for brushing the meat while it is grilled.

5. A half hour before grilling, prepare your gas or charcoal grill to medium-high heat.

6. When the coals are ready, at about 400 degrees with the coals lightly covered with ash, place the marinated leg of lamb on the grill and cook for about 16 minutes per side for medium-rare, 17 minutes for medium. While grilling, brush the remaining marinade on top of the lamb. When finished, transfer the lamb to a large carving board and let rest for 15 minutes, allowing for the meat to properly store its juices.

7. Before serving, slice the lamb into ½-inch-thick diagonal strips. Serve warm.

¾ cup olive oil

¼ cup rosemary leaves, coarsely chopped

3 lemons, juiced

4 garlic cloves, finely chopped

A 6-pound boneless leg of lamb, butterflied

Coarsely ground black pepper

Fresh sea salt

Leg of Lamb with Rosemary-Mustard Marinade

MAKES 4 SERVINGS • ACTIVE TIME: 30 MINUTES • TOTAL TIME: 1 HOUR

The flavors of the rosemary and mustard work well when paired with a leg of lamb. In addition, note that the variation here encourages you to smoke the lamb, allowing for the rich flavor of the mustard to be more pronounced and soulful.

1. In a small bowl, whisk together all of the rosemary-mustard marinade ingredients.

2. Next, place the leg of lamb on a roasting rack. Setting a little aside, rub the marinade on the lamb, massaging it thoroughly into crevices of the meat. Cover the lamb with a sheet of aluminum foil and let stand at room temperature for about 2 hours.

3. A half hour before grilling, prepare your gas or charcoal grill to medium-high heat.

4. When the coals are ready, at about 400 degrees with the coals lightly covered with ash, place the marinated leg of lamb on the grill and cook for about 16 minutes per side for medium-rare, 17 minutes for medium. While grilling, brush the remaining marinade on top of the lamb. When finished, transfer the lamb to a large carving board and let rest for 15 minutes, allowing for the meat to properly store its juices.

5. Before serving, slice the lamb into ½-inch-thick diagonal strips. Serve warm. Consider garnishing with wedges of lemon and parsley leaves.

VARIATION An hour before grilling, take 2 to 3 cups of hickory or oak woodchips and soak them in water. Just before you place the lamb on the grill, scatter the woodchips over the coals. Cover the grill so that the smoke pillows around the meat, and then cook for about 15 minutes for medium-rare.

3 tablespoons olive oil

¼ cup rosemary leaves, finely chopped

¼ cup Dijon mustard

4 garlic cloves, finely chopped

1 large shallot, finely chopped

¼ small lemon, juiced

1 tablespoon flat-leaf parsley, finely chopped

Coarsely ground black pepper

Fresh sea salt

A 6-pound boneless leg of lamb, butterflied

Lamb Chops with Parsley-Mint Sauce

MAKES 4 SERVINGS • ACTIVE TIME: 30 MINUTES • TOTAL TIME: 1 HOUR AND 30 MINUTES

Mint is one of the more frequently used herbs when used with lamb. Parsley and mint complement each other. Be sure to make a little extra of the sauce, as it always seems to go so quickly!

1. In a small bowl, combine the garlic, rosemary, and olive oil. Pour the contents of the bowl onto the lamb chops and then let rest at room temperature for 1 hour.

2. A half hour before grilling, prepare your gas or charcoal grill to medium-high heat.

3. While waiting, in a small bowl, mix together the garlic, parsley, mint, anchovies (optional), and lemon juice. Gradually whisk in the olive oil, and then season with coarsely ground black pepper and fresh sea salt. Transfer to the refrigerator.

4. When the grill is ready, at about 400 to 450 degrees with the coals lightly covered with ash, season one side of the chops with coarsely ground pepper and sea salt. Place the seasoned sides of the chops on the grill at medium heat. Wait 3 minutes until they are slightly charred. A minute before flipping, season the uncooked sides of the chops with the remaining pepper and sea salt. Turn the chops and grill for another 3 minutes for medium-rare, and about 4 minutes for medium. The chops should feel slightly firm if poked in the center.

5. Remove the lamb chops from the grill and transfer to a large cutting board. Let stand for 10 minutes, allowing the lamb to properly store its juices and flavor. Serve warm alongside chilled parsley-mint sauce.

2 garlic cloves

2 tablespoons rosemary, finely chopped

2 tablespoons olive oil

4 lamb chops, about 1¼ inches thick

Coarsely ground black pepper

Fresh sea salt

SAUCE INGREDIENTS

1 garlic clove, finely chopped

1 cup flat-leaf parsley, finely chopped

¼ cup mint leaves, finely chopped

2 anchovies, finely chopped (optional)

¼ small lemon, juiced

½ cup olive oil

Coarsely ground black pepper

Fresh sea salt

Grill-Roasted Rack of Lamb with Garlic-Herb Crust

MAKES 5 TO 6 SERVINGS • ACTIVE TIME: 20 MINUTES • TOTAL TIME: 14 HOURS

Because the rack of lamb is a very delicate meat, be sure to give it the time to marinate overnight. I suggest pairing this with a glass of red wine.

2 tablespoons olive oil

2 garlic cloves, finely chopped

1 teaspoon lemon zest

Two 8-rib racks of lamb, about 1 pound each

Coarsely ground black pepper

Fresh sea salt

GARLIC-HERB CRUST INGREDIENTS

4 garlic cloves, finely chopped

½ small shallot, finely chopped

¼ cup flat-leaf parsley, coarsely chopped

2 tablespoons rosemary, finely chopped

1 tablespoon thyme, finely chopped

1 tablespoon olive oil

Coarsely ground black pepper

Fresh sea salt

1. The night before grilling, combine the olive oil, garlic, and lemon zest in a large sealable plastic bag. Pat dry the racks of lamb, and then season them with coarsely ground black pepper and fresh sea salt, kneading the pepper and salt deeply into the meaty sections of the lamb. Add the racks of lamb into plastic bag and place in the refrigerator. Let marinate overnight.

2. An hour and a half before grilling, remove the racks of lamb from the refrigerator and let rest, uncovered and at room temperature.

3. A half hour before grilling, prepare your gas or charcoal grill to medium heat.

4. While the grill heats, combine all of the ingredients to the garlic-herb crust in a small bowl. Next, take the racks of lamb and generously apply the crust ingredients to it, being sure to apply the majority of the crust on the meaty side of the rack.

5. When the grill is ready, at about 400 degrees with the coals are lightly covered with ash, place the meat-side of the racks of lamb on the grill and cook for about 3 to 4 minutes. When the crusts are browned, flip the racks of lamb and grill for another 5 minutes for medium-rare.

6. Transfer the racks of lamb from the grill to a large carving board and let rest for about 10 minutes before slicing between the ribs. Serve warm.

Marinated Lamb Kebabs with Mint Chimichurri

Marinated Lamb Kebabs with Mint Chimichurri

MAKES 8 TO 10 SERVINGS • ACTIVE TIME: 30 MINUTES •
TOTAL TIME: 5 TO 13 HOURS

Lamb-Kebabs are always a great route to go with when serving at a large gathering. As such, I have double the recipe so that it will provide about 8 to 10 servings. The Mint Chimichurri goes very well with the lamb.

1. The night before you plan to grill, season the lamb cubes with coarsely ground black pepper and fresh sea salt. Set aside.

2. Next, in a large sealable plastic bag (if you need two, divide recipe between both bags), combine the remaining ingredients except for the onion and pepper. Add the lamb cubes to the bag and then transfer to the refrigerator, letting the meat marinate from 4 hour to overnight, the longer the better.

3. An hour and a half before grilling, remove the lamb from the refrigerator and let rest, uncovered and outside of the red wine marinade, at room temperature.

4. In a small food processor, puree the garlic, parsley, mint, shallot, lime juice, and red wine vinegar. Slowly beat in the olive oil, and then remove from the processor. Season with coarsely ground black pepper and fresh sea salt, cover and then set aside.

5. A half hour before grilling, prepare your gas or charcoal grill to medium-high heat.

6. Pierce about four lamb cubes with each bamboo skewer, making sure to align the pieces of onion and pepper in between each cube.

7. When the grill is ready, at about 400 degrees with the coals lightly covered with ash, place the skewers on the grill and cook for about 15 to 20 minutes. Transfer the kebabs to a large carving board and let them rest for 5 minutes before serving with the Mint Chimichurri sauce.

TOOLS

24 bamboo skewers

LAMB INGREDIENTS

2 pounds lamb, cut into 1½-inch cubes

Coarsely ground black pepper

Fresh sea salt

3 tablespoons olive oil

1½ cup red wine

4 garlic cloves, crushed

1 shallot, finely chopped

2 teaspoons rosemary, finely chopped

1 teaspoon ground cumin

2 red onions, cut into square pieces

2 red peppers, cut into square pieces

MINT CHIMICHURRI INGREDIENTS

2 garlic cloves

2 cups flat-leaf parsley

2 cups mint leaves

1 small shallot

¼ small lime, juiced

4 tablespoons red wine vinegar

½ cup olive oil

Coarsely ground black pepper

Fresh sea salt

Lamb Chops with Paprika-Salt Rub

MAKES 4 SERVINGS • ACTIVE TIME: 15 MINUTES • TOTAL TIME: 1 HOUR AND 30 MINUTES

The paprika-salt is a spice both soft and strong at the same time. I suggest serving with a side of Grilled Eggplant (page 272).

1. An hour before grilling, brush the meat on the lamb rib chops with olive oil and let stand at room temperature.

2. In a small bowl, mix together the remaining ingredients to make the paprika-salt rub. Using your hands, generously apply the rub to the lamb rib chops.

3. Prepare your gas or charcoal grill to medium-high heat.

4. When the grill is ready, at about 400 to 450 degrees with the coals lightly covered with ash, place the lamb rib chops on the grill and cook for about 4 minutes or until the spices have browned. Turn the chops and cook for another 3 to 4 minutes for medium-rare, 4 to 5 minutes for medium.

5. Transfer the lamb rib chops to a large carving board and let stand for 5 minutes before serving.

12 lamb rib chops, each about 1 inch thick

2 tablespoons olive oil

2 tablespoons smoked paprika

1 tablespoon cumin seeds

2 teaspoons coriander seeds

½ teaspoon cayenne pepper

Coarsely ground black pepper

Fresh sea salt

Lamb Meatballs in Spicy Tomato Sauce

**MAKES 4 SERVINGS • ACTIVE TIME: 45 MINUTES •
TOTAL TIME: 2 HOURS AND 30 MINUTES**

The lamb meatball is very different than that of the beef. The flavor is much more compact in these meatballs, and as such these meatballs will last for several days afterward. They work both as an appetizer and main course, and after the day of grilling, they work perfectly as a mid-day snack.

1. In a large bowl, mix together the onion, garlic, whisked eggs, cumin, oregano, and cinnamon. Next, knead the lamb into the bowl with your hands, making sure to toss the ingredients throughout the ground lamb. Let rest for 5 minutes and then add in the parsley, pepper, and salt. Let stand at room temperature for 30 minutes.

2. A half hour before cooking, place a cast-iron skillet on your gas or charcoal grill and prepare the grill to medium-high heat. Leave the cast-iron skillet on the grill while heating so that it develops a faint, smoky flavor.

3. Using your hands, firmly form the lamb meat into balls 1½ to 2 inches wide. Place on a platter and set alongside grill.

4. When the grill is ready, at about 400 degrees with the coals lightly covered with ash, add the 2 tablespoons of olive oil into the skillet. When hot, add the meatballs one by one and sear on all sides for about 8 minutes, or until all sides are browned. Remove from skillet and set aside.

5. Next, add the remaining ¼ cup of olive oil to the skillet, scraping off brown bits from the bottom. When the oil is hot, add the garlic and cook until golden, about 30 seconds to 1 minute: Do not let brown. Add the tomatoes, oregano, rosemary, thyme, and the seared meatballs. Simmer for 15 minutes. Next, add the ground cumin, red pepper flakes, wine, basil, pepper, and salt and simmer for 20 more minutes, until the meatballs are cooked through.

6. Remove the cast-iron skillet from the grill and spoon the lamb meatballs and sauce into warmed bowls.

TOOLS
Cast-iron skillet

LAMB INGREDIENTS
1 medium white onion, finely diced
1 garlic clove, minced
2 whole eggs, whisked
1 teaspoon ground cumin
1 teaspoon dried oregano
½ teaspoon ground cinnamon
2 pounds ground lamb
¼ cup flat-leaf parsley, finely chopped
Coarsely ground black pepper
Fresh sea salt

SAUCE INGREDIENTS
¼ cup olive oil, plus 2 tablespoons
3 garlic cloves, minced
28-ounce can whole tomatoes
1 sprig oregano
1 sprig rosemary
1 sprig thyme
½ teaspoon ground cumin
1 teaspoon red pepper flakes
¼ cup dry white wine
Handful of fresh basil leaves
Coarsely ground black pepper
Fresh sea salt

Pork

When it comes to grilling over open flame or slow roasting in smoky, low temperatures, no other meat stands up to high and low heat better than pork. Whether we're cooking ribs or roasting a loin, pork offers some of the most flavorful dishes that can be prepared on a grill. Interesting too is that it's one of the most forgiving meats.

With more than four hundred breeds of domestic pig raised around the world, farming hog and pig is big business as pork is the most widely consumed meat globally. As is the case with farm-to-table producers, raising pig has also become an artisan trade.

Large-scale pig farms may house as many as four thousand to five thousand pigs. Meanwhile, local, small-scale pig farms are focusing on raising and preserving heritage pork breeds, several of which have been nearly wiped out because they do not hold up well under intense farming practices used by large-scale enterprises. The good news is that local farmers and discerning chefs are working hard at breeding and preparing dishes that accentuate the discerning qualities of heritage pork. And as consumers become more and more aware of the varieties in their pork choices, the demand for heritage pork is increasing.

There is a variety of pork breeds to choose from. Each has its own signature flavors and purposefulness. The Tamworth is known for its flavorful bacon, while the Duroc is known for being the most delectable and moist—perfect for roast loin of pork. If you're interested in finding heritage breeds, seek the advice of local farmers and chefs,

If you don't hesitate to place an order for a fresh harvested turkey before Thanksgiving, it should be no different if you're hoping to achieve spectacular results with pork on the grill. Freshly harvested pork ribs, loin, or chops are unmatched against any other grilled meat. Pork absorbs rubs, seasonings, and the aroma of good hard wood smoke like no other meat, and it is because of these qualities that make it one of the most forgiving meats when it comes to grilling and one of the most widely consumed meat around the world.

Selecting the right cut of pork is essential when cooking over intense heat. This is never more true than with pork chops, largely due by the fact that the average pork chop is often cut far too thin for grilling. If you're looking for single-rib pork chops, we believe you should never stray below a thickness of at least 1½ inches. But for the ultimate experience in pork chops, reach for the double-cut chop. We lean toward the rib chop, and within this category we reach for the center cut and the loin cut chops. The center cut is our preferred cut as we like the balance between pork fat and meat, with the meat being less fatty. (We may be a minority, though. Many chefs and butchers prefer the loin cut chop as there is a slightly heavier balance of fat to meat, which helps in keeping the grilled meat juicy and flavorful.) Whether you love a center cut or a loin cut chop, we recommend a double-cut chop. With this thicker-style chop you gain the extra fat for flavor and the thicker cut of meat that will help keep the grilled chops tender and flavorful. Fat for flavor and protection: More meat, more juices.

Long gone are the days where there was only one proper temperature for cooking pork—and that was well done. Generations of cooks were taught that a shade of pink in cooked port was an open invitation to trichinosis; either it was pure white within or it wasn't ready to be served. Growing up, I'd follow the scent of my father's sautéed pork chops from several houses away. He would cook them on our electric stove in a skillet with onions, salt and pepper. The aroma was intoxicating. The only problem was that my father, John Sr., was all too familiar with what were then considered rules in cooking pork; he'd fry those pork chops until they were cooked straight through, as tough as leather.

Cooking well-seasoned pork a bit too long is not nearly as disastrous as with a New York strip steak or a chicken breast. That's not to say, pork can't be overcooked... But don't ask my father. He would have advised you otherwise.

Basic Grilled Roast Pork Loin

Basic Grilled Roast Pork Loin

MAKES 5 TO 6 SERVINGS • ACTIVE TIME: 1 HOUR AND 15 MINUTES • TOTAL TIME: 2 HOURS

These basic ingredients bring out the natural juices and flavors. Just be sure to use a pan that can go from the oven to the grill.

5 tablespoons of olive oil
1 or 2 sprigs of fresh rosemary
2¼ pounds loin of pork
Fresh sea salt
Coarsely ground black pepper

TIP: FOR ANY OVEN-TO-GRILL RECIPE, AVOID USING ANY COOKWARE THAT HAS A PLASTIC, WOOD, OR SYNTHETIC-TYPE HANDLE. IT IS BEST IF THE PAN HAS ROUNDED SIDES, HIGH ENOUGH TO PREVENT THE OIL FROM SPILLING OR FLARING UP WHEN BASTING.

1. Fire up your grill and allow the coals to settle into a temperature of about 350 degrees. While the grill is heating, slowly sauté the olive oil and rosemary in a cast-iron or All-Clad–style high heat–friendly pan. Be sure the pan is oven-and-grill friendly, as you will be placing this pan directly onto your grill.

2. After the oil and rosemary have been thoroughly heated and the flavors of the sprigs are infused throughout the oil (about 10 to 12 minutes), rub your pork loin with sea salt and fresh cracked pepper to your desired seasoning, and place the pork loin into the pan, turning it so the entire loin is covered with the heated oil.

3. Baste for 5 to 10 minutes at a medium heat until the loin begins to brown. Once your grill has reached the desired temperature, move the entire pan to your grill grate.

4. Cover your grill and allow the pork to cook for 45 minutes, turning and basting the pork occasionally so all sides are thoroughly browned from the heat of the hot pan.

5. At about 45 minutes, remove the pork loin from the pan and place directly on the grate. Continue to baste your pork loin using the infused oil from the pan, turning the loin evenly so the entire roast is meets the heat side of your grill. Baste and turn for an additional 15 or so minutes or until the roast meets your desired temperature.

6. Remove from fire and let the loin rest for 10 to 12 minutes. Carve and serve with sides of your choice.

Grilled Roast Pineapple Pork Loin

**MAKES 5 TO 6 SERVINGS • ACTIVE TIME: 1 HOUR AND 30 MINUTES •
TOTAL TIME: 2 HOURS AND 15 MINUTES**

Here we introduce more exotic flavors with a guest-worthy variation on grilled roast pork loin.

1. Fire up your grill and allow the coals to settle into a temperature of about 350 degrees.

2. While the grill is heating, slowly sauté the olive oil and rosemary in a cast-iron or All-Clad–style high heat-friendly pan. Be sure the pan is oven friendly, as you will be placing this pan directly onto your grill.

3. After the oil and rosemary have been thoroughly heated and the flavors of the sprigs are infused throughout the oil, add in a ½ cup of crushed pineapple, honey, water, and ginger. Stir thoroughly, and bring the mixture to a soft boil.

4. Rub your pork loin with salt and pepper to your desired seasoning, and place the pork loin into the pan, turning it so the entire loin is covered with the basting sauce for 5 to 10 minutes at a medium heat until the loin begins to brown. Once your grill has reached the desired temperature, move the entire pan to your grill grate.

5. Cover your grill and allow the pork to cook for 45 minutes, turning and basting the pork occasionally so all sides are browned from the heat of the hot pan.

6. After about 45 minutes, remove the pork loin from the pan and place directly on the grate. Use the remaining ½ cup of crushed pineapple to baste the loin thoroughly creating a golden brown glaze as you turn the loin for another 15 minutes.

7. Remove from fire and let the loin rest for 10 to 12 minutes. Carve and serve with sides of your choice.

5 tablespoons of olive oil
1 or 2 sprigs of fresh rosemary
1 cup of crushed pineapple
¼ cup of honey
¼ cup of water
**1 teaspoon fresh ground
or grated ginger**
2¼ pounds loin of pork
Fresh sea salt
Coarsely ground black pepper

Grilled Roast Pork with Orange Rind

MAKES 5 TO 6 SERVINGS • ACTIVE TIME: 1 HOUR AND 30 MINUTES • TOTAL TIME: 2 HOURS AND 30 MINUTES

No bland meat here—orange, garlic, chile, and oregano come together beautifully in this grilled roast pork.

3 tablespoons of olive oil

1½ cups of fresh orange juice without pulp (homemade is best)

1 or 2 teaspoons of grated orange rind

1 clove of garlic, chopped

2 bay leaves

Pinch of chili powder

Pinch of dried oregano

2½ pounds pork loin

Fresh sea salt

Coarsely ground black pepper

1. Fire up your grill and allow the coals to settle into a temperature of about 350 degrees.

2. Then, in a grill-friendly sauté pan, heat the olive oil and spread to cover the entire bottom of the pan, once the oil begins to brown, gently pour in the fresh orange juice, adding the grated orange rind, chopped clove of garlic, two bay leafs, pinch of chile powder, and pinch of oregano and stir till the ingredients are heated and mixed thoroughly.

3. Rub your pork loin with sea salt and fresh cracked pepper to your desired taste, and place the pork loin into the pan.

4. Leave the pan on the grate and cover the grill allowing the roast port to cook for about 1½ hours, basting often or at least every 15 to 20 minutes or so.

5. At 1 hour 15 minutes, remove the roast from the pan and place directly on the grill for browning and searing. Continue basting and turning so the pork receives the direct heat evenly on all sides.

6. When the roast has browned and seared, remove it from the grill and allow it to sit for 10 minutes before carving.

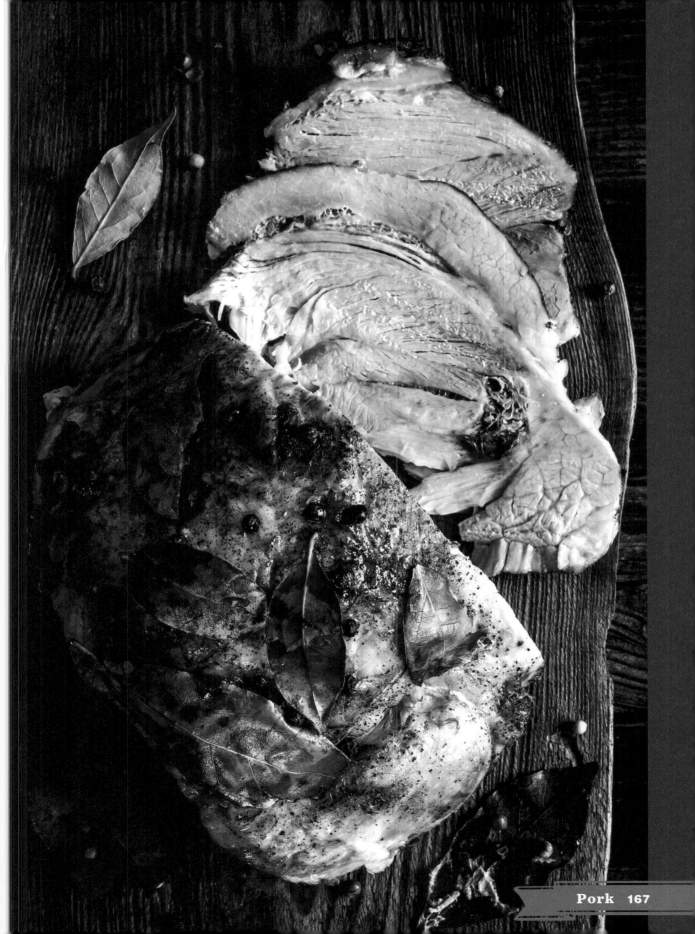

Braised and Grilled Pork with Rosemary

**MAKES 5 TO 6 SERVINGS • ACTIVE TIME: 45 MINUTES •
TOTAL TIME: 1 HOUR AND 45 MINUTES**

My favorite thing about this dish is the way the rosemary needles catch and burn over the grill, bringing a loving charred and sweet flavor to the roast.

1. To enhance the flavor and to prevent the rosemary from searing completely off during the cooking process, push the rosemary needles into the meat. This will help infuse the flavor throughout the pork. Leave a little bit of each rosemary sprig sticking out to catch and burn from the flame; this adds to the flavor.

2. Brush and coat the roast with olive oil.

3. Place the roast into a deep sauté pan that can withstand the direct heat of your grill. Place the remaining oil into the pan, turning and cooking the pork evenly on all sides until it reaches a lovely golden brown.

4. Add the garlic, onion, and remaining rosemary, and let the meat and seasoning cook together for about an hour. If you can control the temperature of your grill, bring the heat down so everything may simmer together for 1½ hours.

5. Just before the pork appears to be done, remove it from the pan and place it directly on the grill to sear off the rosemary sprigs and to gracefully char the exterior to your preference.

6. Remove the roast from the grill, and let it stand for 10 to 12 minutes. Slice thin before serving, and use some of the cooked juices as a light gravy if the pork happens to get slightly overdone.

2 sprigs of rosemary (remove needles from their stems)

2¼ pounds of boneless pork loin

8 tablespoons of olive oil

1 garlic clove, crushed

½ onion, chopped

¾ cup white wine

1 tablespoon white vinegar

Fresh sea salt

Coarsely ground black pepper

TIP: FOR SUMMER FLAVORS, CONSIDER SUBSTITUTING 2 SPRIGS OF ROSEMARY WITH 3 TABLESPOONS FRESHLY CHOPPED DILL.

Basic Grilled Double-Cut Rib Chops

MAKES 4 TO 6 SERVINGS • ACTIVE TIME: 25 MINUTES • TOTAL TIME: 45 MINUTES

I find pork delicious without any rubs, sauces, or marinades. Properly cooked, a great chop will burst with flavor. With this dish, there's no need to overpower the pork. Just sprinkle the chops with a hint of salt and fresh cracked pepper.

4 to 6 double-cut rib chops (one chop per person)

Fresh sea salt

Fresh cracked pepper

TIP: IF YOU DEMAND MORE FLAVOR FROM YOUR PORK, TRY ADDING DIFFERENT HARDWOODS TO YOUR FIRE (OR INTO A WET CHIP CHAMBER IF COOKING OVER A GAS GRILL). APPLE AND CHERRY WOODS OFFERS A MILD BUT LOVELY FRUIT FLAVOR. IN FACT, MANY FINE CHEFS PREFER APPLE WOOD FOR SMOKING PORK, BEEF, CHICKEN, OR EVEN FISH.

1. Preheat one side of your grill to 400 degrees. If possible, create a two-zone cooking area: one zone will be your hot zone, concentrating your coals or heat source beneath one side of your grilling area, while the second zone will be arranged on the opposite side of the grill with little to no coals or flame beneath this surface area. Use the hot side to sear your chops, and the cool side to allow your chops to cook through the radiating heat. This will help ensure that your chops do not overcook and dry out.

2. Place the chops directly over the hot zone and sear both sides of the chops until evenly browned, about 5 minutes per side. Keep a watchful eye on the grill during this stage as fat drippings can create flare-ups that will char rather than sear the meat.

3. Once the chops are seared golden brown, move them over to the cooler zone and let them cook more thoroughly and slowly. If using a meat probe thermometer, look for temperatures in the center of your cut from 135 degree for medium rare and approximately 145 degrees for a tender and flavorful medium. Season with salt and pepper.

Blueberry Pork Chops

MAKES 4 TO 6 SERVINGS • ACTIVE TIME: 1 HOUR AND 20 MINUTES • TOTAL TIME: 2 HOURS

Pork goes so well with sweet fruits, and blueberry is no exception!

1. Get your grill started, shooting for a temperature of about 375 to 400 degrees. Meanwhile, dust your chops with almond flour.

2. Melt the clarified butter and olive oil in a saucepan that can withstand the flames of your grill. Add the pork chops and cook over the grill until evenly browned.

3. Add the wine and cook off the alcohol and to reduce the wine so it becomes a nice flavorful stock, adding salt and pepper to your preferred flavor.

4. Mix the blueberries and the honey in a food blender, one that will allow you to easily spatula off the blueberry honey concoction from the bottom and sides of the blender. A food processor works wonders in this situation as it has a nice wide opening.

5. Coat the pork chops with the blueberry-honey mixture and grill them over the open flame to sear in the final flavors, about 5 minutes per side.

6. As the chops have already cooked in the saucepan, they should not need more than a minute or two on each side before being ready to serve. We always try to let our meats and chops stand for about 10 minutes before serving.

4 to 5 spare rib pork chops
Almond flour (or other Paleo flour)
2 tablespoons clarified butter
3 tablespoons of olive oil
¾ cup of red wine
Salt and pepper, to taste
2¾ cups of blueberries
½ cup of honey

Killer BBQ Spare Ribs

MAKES 6 TO 8 SERVINGS • ACTIVE TIME: 1 HOUR AND 45 MINUTES • TOTAL TIME: 4 TO 5 HOURS

Without approaching the task via a day-long, low heat smoking process, we tackle our ribs a little bit more conventionally (and much more simply): We first slow roast our ribs in the oven at a low temperature of 200 degrees for about 3 hours. This allows the acids and seasonings to gently tenderize the meat, while the low heat loosens the meat from the bone so the cooked rib meat will pull away without fuss. We use a covered turkey roasting pan. The cover keeps the moisture inside the roasting pan, which helps the seasoning seep into the meat and tenderizes too. And our pan is long enough to keep the full rack of ribs intact for easier grilling.

1. Preheat the oven to 325 degrees. Meanwhile, mix the BBQ sauce ingredients—all the ingredients except the ribs themselves—in a large sauce pan over low to medium heat allowing the sugars to melt. Line the bottom the roasting pan with a thick layer of the BBQ sauce.

2. Place each rack of ribs into the roasting pan, layering them with a solid basting of the sauce so both sides of each rack of ribs are fully coated. Cover and allow the ribs to cook for 2½ to 3 hours. No need to turn or recoat the ribs during this process.

3. About 15 to 20 minutes before the ribs have finished cooking in your oven, fire up your grill. A gas grill will work just fine, but there's nothing better than wood-grilled BBQ ribs so consider your options carefully! Look to achieve a medium heat from your grill.

4. Use long tongs that will allow you to slide the tong the full length of the rack of ribs. This will help prevent the ribs from breaking off as the ribs will be soft and tender from their time in the oven.

5. Basting is perhaps the most important final step in preparing killer ribs. I continually baste the ribs, always trying to achieve a beautiful dark brown and black glazed surface. As soon as the flames char an edge of the meat, I quickly baste over that area with a fresh coat of sauce and turn the ribs so the opposite side can be lightly and evenly charred by the fire as well. Unlike steaks on the grill, I turn the ribs over and over, basting and turning each rack in order to achieve the best and most flavorful results. Do not worry about a little bit of blackening and charring; paint over all the charred areas with a fresh coat of BBQ sauce and the two flavors wed together beautifully.

6. As soon as the ribs reach the level of browning and blackening you desire, remove the ribs from the grill and place them onto a serving tray. Do not place them back into the roasting pan. Bring the ribs directly to the table and allow them to cool to touch before digging in.

2 or 3 cloves of garlic, sliced extra thin

1 clove of crushed or minced garlic

1 cup of local honey

⅓ cup of dark molasses

⅓ cup of local dark maple syrup

1½ tablespoons of paprika

1 teaspoon sea salt

1½ teaspoons of fresh ground pepper

1 tablespoon chili ancho powder (add more if you like your BBQ extra spicy)

2 teaspoons of ground cumin

½ cup of apple cider vinegar (the more you add, the tangier the flavor)

1½ cups of organic strained tomatoes

5 or 6 ounces of organic tomato paste (no sugar added)

¼ cup of chili sauce

¼ cup of Worcestershire sauce

1½ tablespoons of fresh squeezed lemon juice

5 tablespoons of chopped onions

1 teaspoon mustard powder

½ pineapple, cubed (if fresh juice collects on your cutting board, add that in too!)

4 to 5 pounds of baby back pork ribs

TIP: THE MORE LAYERS OF SAUCE, THE RICHER THE TASTE AND THE MORE GRATIFYING THE DINING EXPERIENCE.

Paleo Pork Porchetta

MAKES 4 TO 6 SERVINGS • ACTIVE TIME: 1 HOUR AND 30 MINUTES •
TOTAL TIME: 4 HOURS

We first experienced Italian pork porchetta sandwiches in a small market outside the center of Siena, Italy. The flavors were outstanding. And so we needed to recreate this amazing dish Paleo-style. We recommend grilling the pork over apple wood to add that wonderful smoked flavor to an already extraordinarily tasty recipe.

1. Allow the pork to achieve room temperature. Season the pork shoulder with salt and pepper to taste.

2. In a large sauce pan, heat the olive and the oil from the anchovies together over high heat. Toss in the garlic and onions and cook until they are near brown. Stir in the rosemary, crushed red pepper, fennel seeds, the zest of 1 orange and 1 lemon, and only 3 or 4 fillets of anchovies. Use a wood spatula and break down the anchovy fillets as you stir and mix the ingredients creating your marinade. About a minute before you remove the sauce pan from the grill or stovetop, pour in the freshly squeezed orange juice and stir so the sweet citric flavor merges throughout. Remove the pan and allow this concoction to cool to room temperature.

3. Season the bottom of a glass casserole dish with the marinade and rest the pork shoulder into this dish. Use the remaining marinade to completely cover the pork shoulder, spreading and massaging the marinade into the various nooks and crannies of the meat. Cover the dish and refrigerate for the night.

4. Remove the marinated pork from the refrigerator several hours before you plan to cook. Allow the marinated pork to achieve room temperature once more. Meanwhile, fire up your grill to about 300 to 400 degrees.

5. Place your pork shoulder directly on the preheated grill, pouring the excess marinade over it so the full flavors of the marinade can be cooked onto the pork. (For health reasons, do NOT use this marinade later in the cooking process for basting; the marinade has had raw meat soaking in it, and it needs to cook just as the meat does.)

6. Cook the shoulder for about 6 to 8 minutes on either side, closing the grill so the smoke and heat will work together in an oven-like manner.

7. Once you're satisfied that the pork has reached your desired temperature level (about 145 degrees for medium) remove the pork and allow it to cool for 10 to 15 minutes before slicing it thinly. Serve warm.

2½- to 3-pound boneless pork shoulder, butterflied

½ cup of sea salt

½ cup of freshly ground black pepper

2 or 3 tablespoons olive oil

Small tin of olive oil–packed anchovies (use the oil)

4 cloves of garlic, thinly paper thin

1 medium-size onion, chopped

Needles from 1 or 2 sprigs of rosemary

2½ tablespoons crushed red pepper

1½ tablespoons fennel seeds

2 oranges (zest one completely; save the other to grill)

1 lemon (zest the entire rind)

TIP: While the pork is marinating, turn it over at least once, making sure the marinade is equally distributed.

Poultry

Poultry is only second to pork in its popularity worldwide. As a category of meat, poultry may offer some of the most extreme ranges of flavor. Compared to chicken, the most fundamental meat within the poultry family, duck and quail are considered to be much more oily with a higher fat content, very much like the dark meat of chicken legs. Turkey lies somewhere in between, boasting both a hearty white meat, as well as very dense thighs and legs. It is extremely important to understand the qualities of each bird within the poultry family before setting out to prepare a meal altogether. The recipes ahead are some of my favorites. In fact, when I approached this project, I considered expanding this chapter into its own stand-alone book, one of the reasons being the diversity of stock in the poultry family.

A dish that still tantalizes me even in my memory was a skin-on chicken breast prepared by Chef Derek Bissonnette at the renowned White Barn Inn in my hometown of Kennebunkport, Maine. Derek's classic, delicate approach to preparing the chicken kept the meat moist and succulent even after it had been roasted over high heat. The strong flavors in the charred-grill skin balanced elegantly with those of the tender meat. As I learned from Derek, when it comes to grilling any type of poultry, it is essential to marinate, baste, or butterfly the bird so that it does not overcook and become too tough.

All in all, poultry is a very versatile meat, although it can take a little while to be familiar with grilling it. The recipes found in this chapter serve chicken in eleven different ways—from milder flavors like Grilled Lemon and Garlic Chicken (page 205) to barbecue favorites such as Smoked Pulled Barbecue Chicken Sandwiches (page 192) with Paleo buns (page 126). I've also picked a variety of recipes for heat lovers—with dishes inspired by Mexican, Indian, and Asian food traditions. Jamaican Jerk Chicken with Grilled Pineapples (page 186) is one of my fiery favorites. And to really impress your guests with your grilling skill, try the classic Chicken Under Brick with Cilantro Oil (page 196).

From chicken, we turn to a couple of unusual turkey recipes, one being my father's Brined and Grill-Roasted Turkey we enjoy on Thanksgiving (page 207). Requiring extra care and vigilance, the brining of the turkey gives the meat a rounder flavor that extends across all parts of the meat. I then move on to the Cajun Turkey with Cranberry Sauce (page 210), perfect for taking leftovers up a notch.

Finally, I present game-oriented recipes such as the Cider-Glazed Cornish Hens (page 212) and Grilled Quail on Citrus Spinach with Toasted Pine Nuts (page 215). As mentioned throughout the book, I encourage you to find the flavors you enjoy, then make them yours.

Red Wine-Marinated Chicken with Chipotle Cauliflower

MAKES 4 TO 5 SERVINGS • ACTIVE TIME: 1 HOUR AND 30 MINUTES • TOTAL TIME: 9 HOURS

For the marinade, be sure to let the bird soak for up to 6 hours, the longer the better. As for the chipotle cauliflower, if you would like to add a smoky flavor, throw some soaked woodchips over the coals and grill with the lid covered.

CHICKEN INGREDIENTS

½ cup olive oil

½ small white onion, finely chopped

¼ cup flat leaf parsley, finely chopped

2 sprigs rosemary, leaves removed and minced

2 garlic cloves, crushed

2 tablespoons red wine vinegar

A 4- to 5-pound chicken

Coarsely ground black pepper

Fresh sea salt

CAULIFLOWER INGREDIENTS

2 large heads cauliflower, cut into florets

¼ cup olive oil

½ lime, juiced

3 garlic cloves, diced

1 tablespoon chipotle powder

2 teaspoons paprika

2 tablespoons basil leaves, sliced

Coarsely ground black pepper

Fresh sea salt.

1. In a large bowl, combine the olive oil, onion, parsley, rosemary, garlic, and vinegar and mix thoroughly. Add the chicken skin-side down into the marinade; keep in mind that the chicken will not be fully submerged. Let soak for 4 to 6 hours, turning the chicken with 1 hour remaining.

2. Remove the chicken from the marinade and season with pepper and salt. Let the chicken stand at room temperature for 30 minutes to 1 hour. A half-hour before grilling, prepare your gas or charcoal grill to medium heat.

3. While waiting, mix the cauliflower florets, olive oil, and lime juice in a medium bowl. Stir in the remaining ingredients. Transfer into a small frying pan. Set aside.

4. When the grill is ready, at about 400 degrees with the coals lightly covered with ash, place the chicken on the grill, skin side up. Cover the grill and cook for about 40 minutes. Before flipping, brush the top of the chicken with the remaining tablespoon of olive oil. Turn and cook for about 15 more minutes until the skin is crisp and a meat thermometer, inserted into the thickest part of the thigh, reads 165 degrees.

5. Remove the chicken, transfer to a large cutting board, and let stand for 15 minutes.

6. Position the aluminum pan of cauliflower on the grill and cover with lid. Cook for 8 to 9 minutes until the florets are crisp with the chipotle powder. Remove from grill and serve alongside the chicken.

Grilled Chicken with Arugula and Balsamic-Rosemary Vinaigrette

**MAKES 4 SERVINGS • ACTIVE TIME: 25 MINUTES •
TOTAL TIME: 2 HOURS AND 30 MINUTES**

While grilling, baste the chicken thighs with the remaining marinade and be sure to keep the grill covered, allowing the skin to cook to a crisp. Serve this with a pinot noir or a Chianti.

1. Combine the chicken thighs, lemon juice, Dijon mustard, 2 rosemary sprigs, garlic, and the 4 tablespoons of olive oil in a large sealable plastic bag. Seal and firmly mix with your hands. Let rest at room temperature for 2 hours.

2. A half hour before grilling, prepare your gas or charcoal grill to medium-high heat.

3. Add the remaining sprig of rosemary and the ½ cup of olive oil into a small saucepan and set over medium-high heat. Bring to a simmer and then remove from heat. Discard the sprig of rosemary and pour the oil into a small bowl. Set aside.

4. When the coals are ready, at about 400 degrees with the coals lightly covered with ash, remove the chicken from the marinade and season with coarsely ground pepper and sea salt. Then, place the chicken thighs skin side down on the grill, and let cook for about 9 minutes. Flip and cook for 4 to 5 more minutes. When finished, the chicken thighs should feel springy if poked with a finger.

5. Remove the chicken thighs from grill and place on a large cutting board. Let rest for 5 to 10 minutes.

6. While waiting, mix the balsamic vinegar and red pepper flakes into the rosemary oil. Season with pepper and salt. Drizzle over arugula and plate evenly. Position chicken thighs on top of arugula salad and garnish with lemon wedges.

8 bone-in, skin-on chicken thighs

1 lemon, ½ juiced and
½ sliced into wedges

2 tablespoons Dijon mustard

3 sprigs rosemary,
leaves removed from 2

1 garlic glove, finely chopped

½ cup, plus 4 tablespoons olive oil

2 tablespoons balsamic vinegar

¼ teaspoon red pepper flakes

Coarsely ground pepper

Fresh sea salt

4 cups arugula, stemmed

Jamaican Jerk Chicken with Grilled Pineapple

MAKES 4 SERVINGS • ACTIVE TIME: 45 MINUTES • TOTAL TIME: 26 HOURS

This is one of my favorite meals. The jerk spice on the chicken is intense and fiery and is not for the timid. The Jamaican Jerk Chicken is just as good when served chilled the next day. If you make a sandwich of it, be sure to use a Paleo-friendly buns (page 126).

1. Combine all the ingredients except for the chicken in a food processor and blend into a marinade. Remove the marinade and place into a large sealable plastic bag. Add the chicken thighs and legs, making sure they are fully submerged in the marinade. Refrigerate for 24 to 48 hours.

2. Soak the woodchips in water for 1 to 2 hours.

3. Remove the bag from the refrigerator 1 hour before grilling. Transfer the chicken thighs and legs from the marinade onto a plate and let rest, uncovered, at room temperature for about 1 hour.

4. A half hour before grilling, prepare your gas or charcoal grill to medium heat. Designate two separate heat sections on the grill, one for indirect heat and the other for direct heat. To do this, simply arrange the coals toward one side of the grill.

5. While waiting, season the pineapple rings lightly with coarsely ground black pepper and fresh sea salt, the transfer aside the grill.

6. When the grill is ready, at about 350 to 400 degrees with the coals lightly covered with ash, remove the woodchips from the water and scatter over the coals. Place the pineapple rings over the cool side of the grill and cook for about 3 to 4 minutes on each side. When golden, remove from grill.

7. Place the chicken thighs and legs skin-side down on the grill over direct heat. Cover with the lid and grill for 6 to 7 minutes. Flip and move the thighs to the cool side of the grill. Cover again and grill for 4 to 5 more minutes. When finished, the chicken should feel springy if poked with a finger.

8. Remove the chicken from the grill and transfer to a large cutting board. Let rest for about 5 minutes, and then serve with the cooled pineapple.

TOOLS
2 to 3 cups hickory or oak woodchips

JERK CHICKEN INGREDIENTS
1 large yellow onion, halved

4 to 5 habeñero chiles, stemmed and seeded

3 scallions

1 2-inch piece of ginger, peeled

8 garlic cloves

1 teaspoon ground cinnamon

1 teaspoon ground nutmeg

2 teaspoons allspice

1 teaspoon dried thyme

1 teaspoon cayenne

¼ teaspoon ground cloves

2 teaspoons coarsely ground black pepper

2 teaspoons fresh sea salt

½ small lime, juiced

½ cup olive oil

1½ cups warm water

4 bone-in, skin-on chicken thighs

4 skin-on chicken legs

PINEAPPLE INGREDIENTS
1 pineapple, peeled, cored and cut into 1-inch thick rings

1 teaspoon dried thyme

Coarsely ground black pepper

Fresh sea salt

Grilled Ginger-Sesame Chicken

MAKES 4 SERVINGS • ACTIVE TIME: 40 MINUTES • TOTAL TIME: 1 HOUR AND 30 MINUTES

This summertime dish is fabulous served outside on your porch or patio. Serve with Grilled Shishito Peppers (page 260).

1. Heat the olive oil in a small skillet over medium-high heat. When hot, add the ginger, onion, garlic, and lemon juice and sauté for about 2 to 3 minutes, or until the onions are translucent and the garlic is crisp but not browned. Remove from heat and transfer to a small bowl.

2. Rub the chicken breasts with pepper and salt and put them in a medium sealable plastic bag. Add the ginger-onion mixture and press around the chicken breasts. Seal and let rest at room temperature for 30 minutes.

3. Prepare your gas or charcoal grill to medium-high heat.

4. In a small dish, mix ½ teaspoon olive oil with sesame seeds. Set aside.

5. When the grill is ready, about 400 to 450 degrees with the coals lightly covered with ash, place the chicken on the grill and sprinkle the tops with half of the oiled sesame seeds. Grill the chicken breasts for about 7 minutes. Flip and season with the remaining sesame seeds, and then grill for 5 to 6 more minutes. When finished, they should feel springy if poked with a finger.

6. Remove and let rest for 5 minutes. Serve warm.

2 tablespoons, plus ½ teaspoon olive oil

1- to 2-inch piece ginger, peeled and sliced

2 green onions, finely chopped

2 garlic cloves, minced

½ small lemon, juiced

4 boneless chicken breasts, about 1½ to 2 pounds

Coarsely ground black pepper

Fresh sea salt

3 tablespoons sesame seeds

Indian-Rubbed Chicken with Mango-Avocado Salad

MAKES 4 TO 5 SERVINGS • ACTIVE TIME: 40 MINUTES • TOTAL TIME: 2 HOURS

This dish is simpler than you'd think. When serving, place the chicken drumsticks over the Mango-Avocado Salad and serve warm.

1. Wash and dry the chicken drumsticks and wings and then rub with olive oil. Let rest at room temperature for about 30 minutes.

2. In a small roasting pan, combine the remaining ingredients and spread evenly along the bottom of the pan. Take the chicken drumsticks and wings and generously rub with the spices. Set aside and let rest for about 1 hour.

3. A half hour before grilling, prepare your gas or charcoal grill to medium heat.

4. When the grill is ready, at about 400 degrees with the coals lightly covered with ash, place the drumsticks and wings on the grill and season the tops with the remaining spices. Grill for about 30 minutes, rotating onto each side.

5. While the chicken is cooking, combine the mango, avocado, red onion, tomatoes, and basil and mix well. Next, add the lemon or lime juice and olive oil and mix lightly. Season with pepper and salt and set aside.

6. Remove the drumsticks and wings from the grill when the skins are crispy and charred. Let rest for 5 minutes and then serve alongside the mango-avocado salad.

CHICKEN INGREDIENTS

6 to 8 chicken drumsticks and wings, about 3½ pounds (or chicken thighs, if preferred)

3 to 4 tablespoons olive oil

1 medium yellow onion, finely chopped

2 scallions, finely chopped

½ small lemon or lime, juiced

3 garlic cloves, minced

3 teaspoons garam masala

½ teaspoon dried thyme

1 teaspoon ground turmeric

1 teaspoon cayenne pepper

Coarsely ground black pepper

Teaspoon fresh sea salt

SALAD INGREDIENTS

2 medium mangos, cubed

2 large avocados, halved, pitted and cubed

¼ small red onion, coarsely chopped

2 cups chopped tomatoes

1 cup basil leaves, thinly sliced

½ small lemon or lime, juiced (use from ingredients above)

1 tablespoon olive oil

2 teaspoons coarsely ground black pepper

1 teaspoon fresh sea salt

Smoked Pulled Barbecue Chicken Sandwiches

Smoked Pulled Barbecue Chicken Sandwiches

MAKES 4 TO 6 SERVINGS • **ACTIVE TIME: 40 MINUTES** • **TOTAL TIME: 10 HOURS**

To get the perfect "pulled" and "shredded" texture to the chicken and still achieve the smoked flavor, simply grill the chicken at first and then quickly braise it in a cast-iron skillet on the grill at medium heat.

1. Combine the rub ingredients for the chicken in a large bowl and then add the chicken breasts. Rub the spices over the chicken and then place the bowl in the refrigerator. Let marinate for 2 to 12 hours, the longer the better.

2. One hour before grilling, add the woodchips into a bowl of water and let soak. At the same time, prepare your gas or charcoal grill to medium heat. Leave the skillet on the grill while heating so that it develops a faint, smoky flavor.

3. When the grill is ready, at about 350 to 400 degrees with the coals lightly covered with ash, scatter half of the woodchips over the coals and then place the chicken breasts on the grill. Cover the grill, aligning the air vent away from the woodchips so that their smoke rolls around the chicken breasts before escaping. Cook for about 7 to 8 minutes on each side and then remove from grill. Transfer the chicken to a large cutting board, let rest for 5 minutes, and then shred the chicken with two forks. Set aside.

4. Scatter the remaining woodchips over the coals and add the clarified butter into the skillet. When hot, add the garlic, onion, and shallot and sauté until the garlic is golden and the onion and shallot are translucent. Add the remaining ingredients and simmer or about 15 minutes, or until the barbecue sauce has thickened. Mix in the chicken and reduce heat. Cook for 5 more minutes and then remove from heat.

5. Let the chicken rest for 5 minutes, allowing the chicken to properly absorb the sauce, and then serve on warm buns.

TOOLS

2 to 3 cups hickory or oak woodchips

Cast-iron skillet

CHICKEN INGREDIENTS

1 teaspoon chili powder

¼ teaspoon cayenne pepper

2 teaspoons Tabasco

½ teaspoon chipotle chile powder

2 to 3 pounds skinless, boneless chicken breasts

6 buns (see Hamburger Bun Recipe, page 126)

SAUCE INGREDIENTS

2 tablespoons clarified butter

4 garlic cloves, finely chopped

½ cup white onion, minced

½ medium shallot, finely chopped

¾ cup tomatoes, crushed

1 cup apple cider vinegar

2 tablespoons honey

Coarsely ground black pepper

Fresh sea salt

Chicken Under Brick with Cilantro Oil

MAKES 4 TO 5 SERVINGS • ACTIVE TIME: 1 HOUR • TOTAL TIME: 2 HOURS

This is a classic style of chicken that involves first butterflying the whole chicken, and then cooking it skin side up with a brick, wrapped in aluminum foil, resting on top. The brick will not only allow for the chicken to be cooked through perfectly but also charred crispy skin.

1. To butterfly the chicken, place the chicken skin-side down on a large cutting board. Then, using a strong set of kitchen shears, cut along the backbone and then remove it. Next, flip over the chicken and flatten the breastbone by pressing it down with your palm.

2. Rub the oil on the chicken and then season with the coarsely ground pepper and sea salt. Let the chicken stand at room temperature for 30 minutes.

3. Prepare your gas or charcoal grill. When cooking this dish, you want to designate two separate heat sections on the grill, one for direct-heat and the other for indirect-heat. To do this, simply arrange the coals toward one side of the grill.

4. When the grill is ready, at about 350 to 400 degrees with the coals lightly covered with ash, place the chicken skin-side down over indirect heat. Lay the two bricks across the chicken and grill until the skin is crisp, about 25 to 30 minutes. Next, using tongs or thick oven mitts, remove the bricks from the chicken and set aside. Flip the chicken and lay the bricks on top. Cover the grill and cook for another 20 minutes until the skin is crisp and a meat thermometer, inserted into the thickest part of the thigh, reads 160 degrees.

5. Transfer the chicken to a large carving board and let rest for 10 to 15 minutes.

6. While waiting, gather the cilantro oil ingredients and add the cilantro, garlic, and lime juice into a food processor. Blend into a paste and then slowly add the olive oil until you reach a consistency you prefer.

7. Carve the chicken and lightly drizzle with the cilantro oil.

TOOLS
2 bricks wrapped with aluminum foil

CHICKEN INGREDIENTS
A 4- to 5-pound whole chicken

2 tablespoons olive oil

2 tablespoons coarsely ground pepper

2 tablespoons fresh sea salt

CILANTRO OIL INGREDIENTS
2 bunches of fresh cilantro, leaves removed

2 garlic cloves, minced

1 small lime, juiced

¼ to ½ cup olive oil

Basil Chicken Breasts with Chile Oil

MAKES 4 SERVINGS • ACTIVE TIME: 20 MINUTES • TOTAL TIME: 6 TO 24 HOURS

While the chicken itself has a soft, basil flavor, the chile oil always comes in with a semi-strong burst of heat. To be safe, serve the chile oil on the side. Serve with several Grilled Cubanelle Peppers (page 262).

1. Add chile peppers into a small saucepan over medium-high heat. Lightly toast until the skin is blackened, about 3 to 4 minutes. Remove the chile and set aside. Next, add the ½ cup olive oil to the saucepan and heat. Mix in garlic and coriander and cook for 4 to 5 minutes. Then add the chile and cook for 4 more minutes. Remove and let rest overnight. (You can store the chile oil up to 4 months. Though, keep in mind that the longer the chile infuses into the oil, the hotter it will be!)

2. Mix the basil leaves, scallions, garlic, and chile pepper in a large bowl, and then add olive oil. Add the chicken breasts into the marinade and place in the refrigerator. Let soak for at least 4 hours or overnight.

3. Remove from the chile oil from the refrigerator and set aside. Also, transfer the chicken from the marinade to a large cutting board and let rest at room temperature for 30 minutes to 1 hour. Leave the marinade near the grill.

4. Prepare your gas or charcoal grill to medium-high heat.

5. When the grill is ready, at about 400 to 450 degrees with the coals lightly covered with ash, place the chicken on the grill and cook for about 7 minutes, frequently basting with the marinade. Flip and grill for another 5 to 6 minutes until finished; they should feel springy if poked with a finger.

6. Remove and let rest for 5 minutes. Serve warm with the chile oil drizzled on the side.

CHILE OIL INGREDIENTS

2 chile peppers of your choice

¾ cup olive oil

1 garlic clove, crushed

1 teaspoon ground coriander

CHICKEN INGREDIENTS

2 cups fresh basil leaves

3 scallions, chopped

2 garlic cloves

1 chile pepper of your choice, stemmed and coarsely chopped

¼ to ½ cup olive oil

4 skin-on boneless chicken breasts

Coarsely ground black pepper

Fresh sea salt

Cilantro-Lime Chicken Tacos with Spicy Guacamole

MAKES 4 SERVINGS • ACTIVE TIME: 30 MINUTES • TOTAL TIME: 3 TO 24 HOURS

Serve this dish—a personal favorite—on a warm summer night with a glass of sangria made from organic red wine.

1. Combine all the cilantro-lime chicken ingredients into a large sealable plastic back and seal. Rub the marinade around in the bag so that it is evenly distributed across the chicken breasts. Transfer to the refrigerator and let marinate for at least 2 hours or overnight.

2. Remove the chicken from the refrigerator and place, uncovered, on a large cutting board. Let rest for 30 minutes to 1 hour.

3. While waiting, prepare the toppings and place in small, individual bowls so that everyone will be able to pick and choose what they desire! Cover and place on table.

4. A half hour before grilling, prepare your gas or charcoal grill to medium heat.

5. When the grill is ready, about 400 to 450 degrees with the coals lightly covered with ash, place the chicken breasts on the grill and cook for about 7 minutes. When the bottom seems charred, flip the chicken and grill for another 5 to 6 minutes; they should feel springy if poked with a finger.

6. Transfer the chicken from the grill to a large cutting board and let rest for 10 to 15 minutes, allowing the meat to properly store its juices.

7. While the chicken rests, grab your guacamole ingredients and add into a large mortar (a medium bowl will do) and break apart with a pestle or fork. Combine the ingredients coarsely, making sure that there are still medium-sized pieces of avocado remaining.

8. Carve the chicken into small ¼-inch pieces and place into beds of iceberg or butter leaves. Serve with a scoop of guacamole to the side.

CHICKEN INGREDIENTS

¾ cup fresh cilantro, finely chopped

2 limes, grated and juiced

½ cup olive oil

1 teaspoon red pepper flakes

2 teaspoons coarsely ground black pepper

1 teaspoon fresh sea salt

4 to 5 skinless, boneless chicken breasts

GUACAMOLE

2 large Mexican Hass avocados, halved and pitted

½ small lime, juiced

¼ small white onion, finely chopped

¼ to ½ cup cilantro, chopped

1 jalapeño, stemmed, seeded, finely chopped

Coarsely ground black pepper

Fresh sea salt

TOPPINGS

1 head iceberg or butter lettuce, leaves removed

2 to 3 cups cherry tomatoes, quartered

½ white onion, chopped

1 cup Salsa Verde (page 133)

Smoked Ginger Chicken Satay with Almond Dipping Sauce

**MAKES 5 SERVINGS • ACTIVE TIME: 30 MINUTES •
TOTAL TIME: 2 HOURS AND 30 MINUTES**

The smoked ginger chicken is perfect when served with the almond dipping sauce, a strong substitute to the classic peanut sauce. Serve with organic white wine.

TOOLS

2 to 3 cups hickory or oak woodchips

1 bag bamboo skewers

CHICKEN SATAY INGREDIENTS

10 boneless, skinless chicken thighs cut into small strips

A 1- to 2-inch piece of ginger, thinly sliced

2 tablespoons sesame seeds

1 large shallot, finely chopped

3 garlic cloves

1 teaspoon ground coriander

1 chile pepper of your choice, stemmed

2 teaspoons coarsely ground black pepper

1 teaspoon fresh sea salt

¼ cup olive oil

ALMOND DIPPING SAUCE INGREDIENTS

½ cup almond butter

1½ cups coconut milk

1 wedge of lime, juiced

1 tablespoon fish sauce

½ teaspoon coarsely ground black pepper

½ teaspoon fresh sea salt

1. Add all of the chicken satay ingredients into a large sealable plastic bag and seal, making sure that marinade covers the chicken strips. Rub the marinade around the chicken in the bag and transfer to the refrigerator. Let marinate for 2 hours.

2. In a medium bowl, add the woodchips and submerge with water. Let soak for 1 hour.

3. Prepare your gas or charcoal grill to medium heat.

4. Remove the chicken strips from the marinade and pierce with the bamboo skewers. Reserve the marinade and place with the chicken strips alongside the grill.

5. Combine the ingredients for the almond dipping sauce in a small saucepan over medium-high heat and bring to a boil. Let cook for about 3 to 4 minutes until the sauce turns golden brown. Remove from heat and cover with aluminum foil.

6. When the grill is ready, about 400 degrees with the coals lightly covered with ash, scatter the woodchips over the coals. Wait a few minutes for the smoke to build, and then place the skewed chicken strips over the smoke. Cover the grill, aligning the vent away from the coals so that the smoke rolls over the chicken strips, and cook for about 4 minutes on each side.

7. Remove from heat and serve alongside the warm almond dipping sauce.

Grilled Lemon and Garlic Chicken

**MAKES 4 TO 5 SERVINGS • ACTIVE TIME: 1 HOUR AND 15 MINUTES •
TOTAL TIME: 1 HOUR AND 30 MINUTES**

When serving a large group, this dish never fails.

1. Prepare your gas or charcoal grill to medium heat.

2. Place the chicken into a large roasting pan and season its cavity generously with coarsely ground black pepper and fresh sea salt. Take 5 of the lemon halves and put them into the cavity, gently juicing them while doing so. Then, grab the remaining lemon half and rub it across the chicken, squeezing it lightly so that its juices seep into the chicken. Discard this half. Fill the cavity with the 2 halves of the garlic head and the thyme and rosemary, and tie the legs together with the butcher's twine. Let rest for 15 minutes.

3. Take 4 tablespoons of olive oil and massage it over the chicken's skin. Season the outside with additional pepper and salt.

4. When the grill is ready, at about 400 degrees with the coals lightly covered with ash, place the chicken on the grill, skin side up. Cover the grill and cook for about 40 minutes. Before flipping, brush the top of the chicken with the remaining tablespoon of olive oil. Turn and cook for about 15 more minutes until the skin is crisp and a meat thermometer, inserted into the thickest part of the thigh, reads 165 degrees.

5. Remove from grill and place on a large carving board. Let the chicken rest at room temperature for 10 minutes before carving. Serve warm.

TOOLS

1 to 2 feet butcher's twine

INGREDIENTS

A 4- to 5-pound chicken

Coarsely ground black pepper

Fresh sea salt

3 lemons, halved

1 garlic head, halved

1 bunch thyme

1 bunch rosemary

5 tablespoons olive oil

TIP: BEFORE FILLING THE CHICKEN'S CAVITY WITH THE GARLIC, THYME, AND ROSE-MARY, HEAVILY RINSE THE CAVITY WITH A COUPLE CUPS OF ORANGE JUICE AND SALT— AN EASY WAY TO REALLY UP THE FLAVOR AND WOW YOUR GUESTS!

Brined and Grill-Roasted Turkey

Brined and Grill-Roasted Turkey

MAKES 8 TO 10 SERVINGS • ACTIVE TIME: 3 HOURS • TOTAL TIME: 9 TO 24 HOURS

Brining and grilling poultry often go hand in hand, allowing for the meat to retain its juice and stay moist. To brine thoroughly, the bird must soak in a mixture of water and kosher salt for up to 12 hours, the longer the better. At the Whalen house for Thanksgiving, my father always does the traditional turkey in the oven and then this recipe with the rotisserie (optional) on the grill. Without a doubt, this is always the winning turkey. Serve with cranberry sauce (page 210).

1. In a large stockpot, add the turkey and submerge with about 8 cups of water and ½ cup of kosher salt; if you need water, make sure to increase the amount of kosher salt. Let the turkey brine at room temperature for 6 to 12 hours.

2. Remove the turkey and pat dry. Grab the orange halves and squeeze over the turkey and inside its cavity. Next, rub the clarified butter on the turkey's skin and season with coarsely ground black pepper and rosemary.

3. Prepare your gas or charcoal grill to medium-low heat and designate two separate heat sections on the grill, one for direct heat and the other for indirect. To do this, simply arrange the coals toward one side of the grill.

4. When the grill is ready, at about 350 to 400 degrees with the coals lightly covered with ash, place the turkey over indirect-heating and grill for about 2¾ hours. While grilling, you want to replenish the coals and flip the turkey every 45 minutes. Insert a meat thermometer into the thickest part of the thigh; when the turkey is finished, the thermometer should read 165 degrees.

5. Remove the turkey from the grill and cover with aluminum foil. Let rest for 45 minutes to 1 hour before carving.

INGREDIENTS

A 12- to 14-pound turkey

8 cups cold water

½ cup kosher salt

2 oranges, halved

2 tablespoons clarified butter

½ sprig rosemary, leaves removed

Coarsely ground black pepper

Cajun Turkey with Cranberry Sauce

MAKES 8 TO 10 SERVINGS • ACTIVE TIME: 3 HOURS • TOTAL TIME: 10 TO 24 HOURS

This is a great meal when cooking for a large family gathering. Slice the turkey completely after grilling and then set aside the extra meat for turkey and cranberry sandwiches the next day (for the Paleo bun recipe, see page 126).

1. In a large stockpot, add the turkey and submerge with about 8 cups of water; if you need more, make sure to increase the amount of kosher salt. Let the turkey brine at room temperature for 6 to 12 hours.

2. For the cranberry sauce, combine the cranberries, honey, orange juice, and lemon juice in a medium saucepan over medium heat. Simmer for about 15 minutes, until the sauce thickens and the berries have broken apart. Transfer to a bowl and refrigerate overnight.

3. Remove the turkey and pat dry. In a small bowl, mix together the Cajun spices. Spoon the clarified butter over the turkey and distribute evenly, and then rub the spices all around the turkey. Let rest at room temperature for 1 to 2 hours.

4. Prepare your gas or charcoal grill to medium-low heat and designate two separate heat sections on the grill, one for direct-heat and the other for indirect. To do this, simply arrange the coals toward one side of the grill.

5. When the grill is ready, at about 350 to 400 degrees with the coals lightly covered with ash, place the turkey over indirect heating and grill for about 2 to 2½ hours. While grilling, you want to replenish the coals and flip the turkey every 45 minutes. Insert a meat thermometer into the thickest part of the thigh; when finished, the turkey should be at 165 degrees.

6. Remove the turkey from the grill and cover with aluminum foil. Let rest for 45 minutes to 1 hour before carving. Serve alongside cranberry sauce.

CAJUN TURKEY INGREDIENTS

A 12- to 14-pound turkey

8 cups cold water

½ cup kosher salt

2 tablespoons onion powder

2 tablespoons paprika

1 tablespoon cayenne pepper

1 tablespoon garlic powder

1 tablespoon ground oregano

1 tablespoon dried thyme

1 tablespoon coarsely ground black pepper

1 tablespoon fresh sea salt

2 tablespoons clarified butter

CRANBERRY SAUCE INGREDIENTS

4 cups raw cranberries

⅓ cup honey

½ cup orange juice

½ small lemon, juiced

Cider-Glazed Cornish Hens

MAKES 4 SERVINGS • ACTIVE TIME: 1 HOUR •
TOTAL TIME: 4 HOURS AND 30 MINUTES

This is main dish for a cool fall evening. Be sure to butterfly the hens beforehand, as this will allow the breasts to cook evenly.

CORNISH HEN INGREDIENTS

Four 1¼-pound Cornish hens, butterflied (see "Chicken Under Brick" recipe, page 196)

Coarsely ground black pepper

Fresh sea salt

¼ cup olive oil

1 sprig thyme, leaves removed

1 sprig tarragon, leaves removed

½ small lemon, juiced

GLAZE INGREDIENTS

1 cup Paleo-friendly apple cider, with no added sugar

1 tablespoon honey

¼ cup clarified butter

1. Season the Cornish hens with coarsely ground black pepper and sea salt. Combine the olive oil, thyme, tarragon, and lemon juice in a small bowl and then place the Cornish hens into the mixture. Let marinate at room temperature for 2 to 4 hours, turning the hens about every 30 minutes so that the marinade coats them evenly.

2. Prepare your gas or charcoal grill to medium-heat and designate two separate heat sections on the grill, one for direct heat and the other for indirect. To do this, simply arrange the coals toward one side of the grill.

3. While waiting for the grill, combine the glaze ingredients in a small saucepan over medium-high heat. Bring the glaze to a boil and reduce to ½ cup, about 10 minutes. Remove from heat and transfer to a small basting bowl.

4. When the grill is ready, about at 400 degrees with the coals lightly covered with ash, brush the glaze over the Cornish hens. Then, place the bird's skin side down over direct heat and cook for 3 minutes. When the skin is a little crispy, flip and move over indirect heat. Cook for about another 25 minutes, basting with the remaining glaze frequently, until the hens are cooked through.

5. Remove the Cornish hens from the grill and transfer to a large carving board. Let rest for 5 to 10 minutes before serving.

Grilled Quail on Citrus Spinach Salad with Toasted Pine Nuts

MAKES 4 SERVINGS • ACTIVE TIME: 20 MINUTES • TOTAL TIME: 2 HOURS

This is a great springtime meal. For the best flavors, be sure to lay the quail on top of the spinach salad with pine nuts. Serve with a glass of white wine.

1. Coat the quail with olive oil and then season with ground pepper and sea salt. Let stand at room temperature for 1 to 1½ hours.

2. While the quail rest, turn to the salad, adding olive oil, vinegar, lime and orange juice, and shallots into a small jar and then seasoning with salt and pepper. In a separate, large bowl, mix the spinach, tomatoes, currants, sunflower seeds, and sesame seeds and set aside. Next, in a small frying pan, heat 1 tablespoon of olive oil and then add the pine nuts. Toast until the pine nuts are brown. Remove from heat and mix into the spinach.

3. Prepare your gas or charcoal grill to medium-high heat.

4. When the grill is ready, at about 400 to 450 degrees with the coals lightly covered with ash, place the quail skin-side up for about 5 minutes until the skin is lightly browned. Flip and grill for 2 more. When finished, transfer quail to a large cutting board and let rest, uncovered, for 5 to 10 minutes.

5. Combine the salad dressing and salad, and then serve with quail.

QUAIL INGREDIENTS

4 to 6 quail, butterflied (see "Chicken Under Brick," page 196)

2 tablespoons olive oil

Coarsely ground black pepper

Fresh sea salt

SALAD INGREDIENTS

½ cup, plus 1 tablespoon olive oil

4 tablespoons white wine vinegar

½ small lime, juiced

¼ orange, juiced

1 small shallot, finely chopped

Coarsely ground black pepper

Fresh sea salt

4 cups baby spinach

½ to 1 cup cherry tomatoes, quartered

4 tablespoons currants

3 tablespoons sunflower seeds

2 tablespoons sesame seeds

½ cup pine nuts

Seafood *and* Shellfish

The Paleo diet revolves around two P's: protein and produce. It is not, as sometimes thought, all about red meat. Presumably, you're eating Paleo for the health benefits, and if that's the case you want to cast a wide net when it comes to your protein sources. In fact, modern science and early civilization comes together in a surprising finding: Micronutrients in seafood, such as omega-3s, are so essential to brain development that it might be yet another reason why so many early peoples were coastal dwellers.

The healthiest—and tastiest—way to make seafood and shellfish a healthy part of your diet is to mix it up, just as you would with fresh produce, getting different nutrients from different sources. This chapter includes recipes for salmon, tuna steaks, red snapper, mahi-mahi, swordfish, scallops, oysters, haddock, trout, flounder, shrimp, mussels, striped bass, and—for a grand finale—Grilled Seafood Stew in Tomato Broth (page 250).

Grilled Salmon over Red Bell Peppers

MAKES 4 SERVINGS • ACTIVE TIME: 25 MINUTES • TOTAL TIME: 50 MINUTES

A classic grilled fillet of salmon is a dish that can often stand by itself due to its fresh flavors. Even so, I recommend serving it over some grilled red bell peppers (maybe add a little asparagus, too) as these complement the flavors of the salmon. Enjoy with a glass of organic white wine.

1. Place the salmon on a large platter and coat evenly with olive oil, coarsely ground black pepper, and salt. Take the lemon half and, holding it in the palm of your hand, squeeze it gently over the salmon. Let rest at room temperature.

2. A half hour before cooking, place a cast-iron skillet on your gas or charcoal grill and prepare to medium heat. Leave the grill covered while heating, as it will add a faint smoky flavor to the skillet.

3. When the grill is ready, at about 400 degrees with the coals lightly covered with ash, add the red bells peppers to the cast-iron skillet and let cook, turning semi-frequently, until the peppers are nearly charred and wrinkled, about 20 minutes. Remove the peppers and let cool.

4. Place the salmon on the grill and cook for about 5 to 6 minutes per side, until the fish is flakey when pierced with a fork. Transfer to a cutting board and let rest for 5 to 10 minutes.

5. Take the peppers and remove the stems and seeds. Next, cut the peppers into long strips and add to a medium bowl. Mix in the olive oil, balsamic vinegar, and thyme and serve alongside the salmon fillets.

SALMON INGREDIENTS

4 salmon fillets, about 4-inch squares

2 tablespoons olive oil

Coarsely ground black pepper

Fresh sea salt

½ lemon

RED BELL PEPPER INGREDIENTS

4 red bell peppers

2 tablespoons olive oil

1 teaspoon balsamic vinegar

1 sprig thyme, leaves removed

Seared Tuna Steaks with Dill Aioli

MAKES 4 SERVINGS • ACTIVE TIME: 25 MINUTES • TOTAL TIME: 50 MINUTES

Seared tuna steaks are always a great on a warm summer evening. When serving these steaks, you have the option of serving chilled or right off the grill. The dill aioli is perfect when served slightly chilled. I recommend serving the steaks with the dill aioli and a side of grilled red peppers.

1. Rub the tuna steaks with a little olive oil and then season with pepper and salt. Let rest at room temperature while you prepare the grill and basil aioli.

2. Prepare your gas or charcoal grill to high heat.

3. While waiting for the grill, combine the dill, parsley, lemon juice, and garlic clove into a small bowl and whisk together. While whisking, slowly incorporate the olive oil and season with fresh sea salt. Set aside or chill in the refrigerator. (If you want a lighter aioli, combine the initial ingredients in a blender and then slowly add the olive oil.)

4. When the grill is ready, at about 450 to 500 degrees with the coals lightly covered with ash, brush the grate with a little olive oil. Tuna steaks should always be cooked between rare and medium-rare; anything over will be tough and dry. To accomplish a perfect searing, place the tuna steaks directly over the hot part of the coals and sear for about 2 minutes per side. The tuna should be raw in the middle (cook 2½ to 3 minutes per side for medium-rare).

5. Transfer the tuna steaks to a large carving board and let rest for 5 to 10 minutes. Slice against the grain and then serve with the dill aioli to the side.

TUNA STEAKS INGREDIENTS

4 fresh tuna steaks, about 2 inches thick

2 tablespoon olive oil, plus a little extra for the grill

Coarsely ground black pepper

Fresh sea salt

DILL AIOLI INGREDIENTS

10 sprigs dill, finely chopped

10 sprigs parsley, finely chopped

¼ small lemon, juiced

1 garlic clove, minced

¾ cup olive oil

Fresh sea salt

Grilled Red Snapper with Chile-Tomato Sauce

MAKES 4 SERVINGS • ACTIVE TIME: 25 MINUTES • TOTAL TIME: 1 HOUR

Red snapper grills well because of its firm texture and mild flavor, and it is complemented by a little bit of heat like in this chile-tomato sauce.

1. Rub the snapper fillets with olive oil and then season with the red pepper flakes, coarsely ground black pepper, and sea salt. Let stand at room temperature while preparing the grill and chile-tomato sauce.

2. A half hour before cooking, place a cast-iron skillet on your gas or charcoal grill and prepare to medium heat. Leave the grill covered while heating, as it will add a faint smoky flavor to the skillet.

3. When the grill is ready, at about 400 degrees with the coals lightly covered with ash, add the chile peppers and cook until the chiles are charred and wrinkled. Remove from pan and transfer to a small cutting board. Let cool and then stem the chiles. Finely chop them and set aside.

4. Add the olive oil to the cast-iron skillet. When hot, add the shallot and garlic cloves and cook until the shallot is translucent and the garlic is golden, about 2 minutes. Add the finely chopped chiles into the pan and sear for 1 minute.
Mix in the tomatoes and cook until they have broken down. Stir in the cilantro, parsley, and chives and sear for a few more minutes. Season with the pepper and salt and transfer to a bowl. While the sauce is still hot, mash with a fork and cover with aluminum foil.

5. Place the seasoned snapper fillets on the grill directly over the heat source. Cover the grill and cook for about 3 minutes per side. When finished, the fillets should be opaque in the center and should easily tear when pierced with a fork. Transfer to a carving board and peel back the skin. Let rest 5 to 10 minutes, and then serve on beds of chile-tomato sauce.

SNAPPER INGREDIENTS]

4 red snapper fillets, skin-on and about 1½ to 2 inches thick

2 tablespoons olive oil

2 teaspoons red pepper flakes (optional)

Coarsely ground black pepper

Fresh sea salt

CHILE-TOMATO SAUCE INGREDIENTS

2 chile peppers of your choice

2 tablespoons olive oil

1 small shallot, finely chopped

2 garlic cloves, minced

2 pounds large tomatoes, crushed

¼ cup fresh cilantro, finely chopped

1 tablespoon flat-leaf parsley, finely chopped

2 tablespoons fresh chives, finely chopped

Coarsely ground black pepper

Fresh sea salt

Grilled Lime Mahi-Mahi and Smoked Green Beans with Prosciutto & Pine Nuts

MAKES 4 SERVINGS • ACTIVE TIME: 45 MINUTES • TOTAL TIME: 2 HOURS AND 30 MINUTES

Because the mahi-mahi has such delicate flavors, it works with nearly any side or marinade. But here we pair it with smoked green beans with prosciutto and pignoli nuts.

MAHI-MAHI INGREDIENTS

½ cup olive oil

½ small lime, juiced

1 garlic clove, minced

1 teaspoon red pepper flakes

½ teaspoon cayenne pepper

4 mahi-mahi fillets

Coarsely ground black pepper

Fresh sea salt

GREEN BEANS WITH PROSCIUTTO & PINE NUTS

2 tablespoons olive oil

3 ounces prosciutto, ⅛ inch thick, sliced into cubes

¼ cup pine nuts

2 to 3 pounds green beans, ends trimmed

2 garlic cloves, finely chopped

¼ small lemon, juiced

Coarsely ground black pepper

Fresh sea salt

1. In a medium roasting pan, combine the olive oil, lime juice, garlic, red pepper flakes, and cayenne pepper and mix thoroughly. Place the mahi-mahi fillets into the marinade and let stand at room temperature for 1 to 2 hours, flipping once.

2. A half hour before cooking, place a cast-iron skillet on your gas or charcoal grill and prepare to medium heat. Leave the grill covered while heating, as it will add a faint smoky flavor to the skillet.

3. When the grill is ready, at about 400 degrees with the coals lightly covered with ash, add the olive oil into the skillet. Wait until very hot, and then add the prosciutto and sear until browned. Next, stir in the pine nuts and toast, about 3 minutes. Stir in the garlic and green beans, then top with lemon juice. Season generously with coarsely ground black pepper and sea salt and cook until the green beans are charred and blistered, about 10 minutes.

4. While the green beans cook, remove the mahi-mahi fillets from the marinade and place directly over the heat source. Cover the grill and cook for about 4 to 5 minutes per side, until the fillets are flakey and moist when touched with a fork.

5. Remove the fillets and green beans from the grill and serve immediately.

Grilled Lemon and Basil Swordfish Steaks with Citrus Salsa

MAKES 4 SERVINGS • ACTIVE TIME: 40 MINUTES • TOTAL TIME: 1 HOUR AND 45 MINUTES

Swordfish is often considered a meat lover's fish. A very filling cut, swordfish is delicious served with this citrus salsa.

1. In a medium bowl, combine the lemon juice, fresh basil leaves, and garlic. Whisk in the olive oil and then let the marinade infuse for 1 hour. Next, rub the oil over the swordfish steaks and then season with coarsely ground black pepper and sea salt. Let stand at room temperature while you prepare the grill and citrus salsa.

2. Prepare your gas or charcoal grill to high heat.

3. While the grill heats, combine the pineapple, cucumber, mango, shallot, red bell pepper, and cilantro in a large bowl. Stir in the lime juice and Tabasco sauce and then season with coarsely ground black pepper and sea salt. Transfer the bowl to the refrigerator and let chill.

4. When the grill is ready, at about 450 to 500 degrees with the coals lightly covered with ash, brush the grate with a little olive oil. Place the swordfish steaks on the grill and then grill for about 3 to 4 minutes per side, until the fish is opaque.

5. Remove the steaks from the grill and place on a large carving board. Let stand for 5 to 10 minutes, and then serve with a side of citrus salsa.

SWORDFISH INGREDIENTS

½ lemon, juiced

¼ cup fresh basil leaves

1 garlic clove, minced

½ cup olive oil, plus extra for the grill

4 swordfish steaks, 1¼ to 1¾ inches thick

Coarsely ground black pepper

Fresh sea salt

CITRUS SALSA INGREDIENTS

1 cup ripe pineapple, diced

¼ cup fresh cucumber, diced

¼ cup ripe mango, diced

1 small shallot, chopped

2 tablespoons red bell pepper, diced

1 tablespoon fresh cilantro, finely chopped

¼ small lime, juiced

½ teaspoon Tabasco sauce

Coarsely ground black pepper

Fresh sea salt

Grilled Peach Scallops with Basil-Cilantro Puree

Grilled Peach Scallops with Basil-Cilantro Puree

**MAKES 4 TO 6 SERVINGS • ACTIVE TIME: 45 MINUTES •
TOTAL TIME: 2 HOURS AND 20 MINUTES**

Scallops have a very delicate flavor. Although they seem very small, scallops are an extremely filling dish and do not require a large side to accompany them, maybe just a small salad or some Grilled Scallions (page 263).

1. In a large bowl, combine the cubed peaches and olive oil. Let rest for about 30 minutes, until the juices from the peaches blanket the bottom of the bowl.

2. Next, season the diver scallops with a little lemon juice, coarsely ground black pepper, and sea salt and then add them into the peach mixture, making sure that most of them are covered. Let the scallops marinate in the refrigerator for 1 to 1½ hours.

3. Prepare your gas or charcoal grill for medium heat, designating 2 sections: one for direct-heat and the other for indirect. To do so, simply pile the coals on one side of the grill.

4. While waiting for the grill, combine the cilantro, basil, parsley, garlic, and jalepeño in a small food processor. Blend into a thick paste, and then gradually add in the lime juice and olive oil until you reach a desired consistency. Season with ground pepper and sea salt, then remove from food processor and set aside.

5. When the grill is ready, at about 400 degrees with the coals lightly covered with ash, place the diver scallops over indirect heat. Cover the grill and cook for about 5 to 6 minutes, flipping once, until the scallops are firm and lightly charred. To check for doneness, insert a fork into the center and if it comes out cold, cook for another minute or so; if it comes out warm, remove the scallops from the grill.

6. Let the diver scallops rest on a carving board for 5 minutes, then plate. Drizzle the basil-cilantro puree over the scallops and to the side. Serve warm.

VARIATION For more heat, use 2 tablespoons finely chopped habanero instead of the jalepeño.

SCALLOP INGREDIENTS

4 large, ripe peaches, cut into ¼-inch cubes

2 tablespoons olive oil

15 u/10 or U-15 diver scallops

Lemon wedge

Coarsely ground black pepper

Fresh sea salt

BASIL-CILANTRO PUREE

½ cup fresh cilantro leaves

½ cup fresh basil leaves

2 tablespoons fresh flat-leaf parsley leaves

2 garlic cloves, minced

2 tablespoons jalapeño, finely chopped

½ small lime, juiced

¼ cup olive oil

Coarsely ground black pepper

Fresh sea salt

TIP: AT FISH MARKETS ESPECIALLY, THEY FREQUENTLY USE U/10 OF U/15 SCALLOPS. THIS SIMPLY MEANS THAT THERE ARE UNDER 10 OR UNDER 15 SCALLOPS PER POUND; IN OTHER WORDS, THE LOWER THE NUMBER, THE LARGER THE SCALLOP.

Oysters with Shallot Mignonette

MAKES 5 TO 6 SERVINGS • ACTIVE TIME: 10 MINUTES • TOTAL TIME: 30 MINUTES

Oysters are light and perfect for socializing. They work as a main course, lunch, or maybe even just a snack. This shallot mignonette takes them up another notch. Serve with white wine.

1. Carefully shuck the oysters and store them in the refrigerator.

2. Next, combine the red wine vinegar, minced shallot, habanero chile, and parsley into a small bowl and then season with coarsely ground black pepper and fresh sea salt. Transfer the bowl to the refrigerator and let the mignonette infuse for 30 to 45 minutes.

3. Remove the oysters from the refrigerator and serve on a platter over finely broken ice. Pour the mignonette into a small bowl. Serve with individual lemon wedges.

24 oysters, freshly shucked

½ cup red wine vinegar

2 tablespoons shallot, minced

½ habanero chile, seeded and finely chopped (optional)

1 teaspoon flat-leaf parsley, finely chopped

Coarsely ground black pepper

Fresh sea salt

1 lemon, sliced into small wedges

Grill-Seared Lemon Haddock with Basil-Walnut Pesto

MAKES 4 TO 5 SERVINGS • ACTIVE TIME: 20 MINUTES • TOTAL TIME: 40 MINUTES

A properly cooked haddock will be flakey with soft flavors. As such, the nutty flavor in the basil walnut pesto works perfectly alongside the haddock.

HADDOCK INGREDIENTS

1½ pound Alaskan haddock fillets

¼ cup olive oil

Coarsely ground black pepper

Fresh sea salt

1 lemon, halved

BASIL WALNUT PESTO

½ cup walnuts

1 bunch basil leaves

1 tablespoon cilantro leaves

2 garlic cloves

½ cup olive oil

Coarsely ground black pepper

Fresh sea salt

1. Place the haddock fillets into a small baking pan and then add the olive oil. Season the fillets with coarsely ground black pepper and sea salt, then with freshly squeezed lemon juice. Let rest at room temperature while preparing the grill.

2. A half hour before cooking, place a cast-iron skillet on your gas or charcoal grill and prepare to medium heat. Leave the grill covered while heating, as it will add a faint smoky flavor to the skillet.

3. While the grill heats, puree the walnuts, basil, cilantro, and garlic cloves in a small food processor. When the mixture is a thick paste, slowly blend in the olive oil until you reach a consistency you like. Remove from food processor, season with black pepper and salt, and set aside.

4. When the grill is ready, at about 400 to 500 degrees with the coals lightly covered with ash, add the fillets into the skillet and sear for about 5 minutes. When the fillets have browned, turn and cook for 1 to 2 more minutes, until the fish is opaque through the center.

5. Transfer the haddock fillets to a carving board and let rest, uncovered, for 5 to 10 minutes. Serve with the basil walnut pesto.

Grilled Trout with Garlic and Herbs

MAKES 4 SERVINGS • ACTIVE TIME: 35 MINUTES •
TOTAL TIME: 1 HOUR AND 10 MINUTES

The flavors of a fillet of grilled trout often depend on the type of water they lived in: The ideal water is cold as the fish will taste very fresh and tender. Lake trout will be a little less tender but still flavorful. Garlic and herbs enhance the flavors of the trout.

½ cup olive oil

4 garlic cloves, finely chopped

2 tablespoons white wine vinegar

¼ small lemon, juiced

2 teaspoons fresh rosemary

1 teaspoon fresh sage

½ teaspoon fresh thyme

8 trout fillets, about 2 pounds

Coarsely ground black pepper

Fresh sea salt

1. Add the olive oil into a small saucepan over medium-high heat. When hot, stir in the garlic and cook until golden, about 2 minutes. Stir in the white wine vinegar, lemon juice, rosemary, sage, and thyme into a small bowl and simmer for 1 minute. Remove and let infuse for 30 minutes.

2. Place the trout fillets into a large baking dish and cover with the garlic and herb oil; if the mixture doesn't cover the fillets, make note and flip halfway during marinating. Transfer the dish to the refrigerator and let the fillets rest in the oil for 30 to 45 minutes.

3. Prepare your gas or charcoal grill to medium-high heat.

4. When the grill is ready, at about 400 to 500 degrees with the coals lightly covered with ash, remove the fillets from the garlic and herb marinade and season with coarsely ground black pepper and sea salt. Place the fillets on the grill, skin side down, and cook for about 2 to 3 minutes per side. Transfer the steaks from the grill to a large carving board and let rest for 10 minutes. Serve warm.

Grilled Flounder with Bacon-Wrapped Asparagus

**MAKES 6 SERVINGS • ACTIVE TIME: 30 MINUTES •
TOTAL TIME: 1 HOUR AND 15 MINUTES**

Grilled flounder is a delicate fish that breaks evenly with your fork. This side of bacon-wrapped asparagus supports the mild flavors of the flounder. Serve with white wine.

1. Season the flounder fillets with coarsely ground black pepper and fresh sea salt and place each fillet on separate sheets of aluminum foil. Divide the clarified butter and dry white wine evenly across the fillets, and then do the same with the tomato, white onion, and garlic. Top each fillet with 2 sprigs of thyme, and then fold the bottom-half of the aluminum foil over the top, forming a tight crease along the side of the flounder.

2. Preheat your gas or charcoal grill to medium-high heat.

3. On a large carving board, arrange the asparagus into groups of 4 or 5. Spread the bacon strips apart, and then move each asparagus group onto the end of 1 strip of bacon. Pull the asparagus tightly together, piling some on top of the others, and then roll the bacon strip around it. When rolled tight, either pierce through the center with a long toothpick, or tie with butcher's twine. Set beside the grill.

4. When the grill is ready, at about 450 to 500 degrees with the coals lightly covered with ash, place the sealed flounder fillets on the grill and cover the grill and cook for about 9 minutes, flipping once, until the flounder fillets feel firm when poked with a finger. Transfer to a large carving board and let rest, their packets discarded, for 10 to 15 minutes.

5. While the flounder rests, place the bacon-wrapped asparagus on the grill and cook until the bacon and the asparagus are both charred, about 5 to 10 minutes.

6. Remove the bacon-wrapped asparagus from the grill and plate alongside flounder fillets. Garnish with wedges of lemon.

TOOLS

Handful of long toothpicks, or 1 to 2 feet butcher's twine

4 sheets aluminum foil

FLOUNDER INGREDIENTS

4 large flounder fillets

Coarsely ground black pepper

Fresh sea salt

4 tablespoons clarified butter

4 teaspoons dry white wine

1 small tomato, seeded and diced

2 small white onions, finely chopped

2 garlic cloves, sliced

8 sprigs thyme

1 small lemon, sliced into wedges

BACON-WRAPPED ASPARAGUS

1½ pounds asparagus, cut to 4-inch pieces

4 to 6 slices of thick bacon

2 tablespoons olive oil

Coarsely ground black pepper

Spicy Shrimp

MAKES 4 TO 6 SERVINGS • ACTIVE TIME: 15 MINUTES • TOTAL TIME: 35 MINUTES

This fiery dish is one of my father's recipes—a summertime favorite. Have plenty of water and napkins on hand.

1. Combine all the spices into a small bowl and mix well.

2. Place the peeled and deveined shrimp into a large bowl and toss with olive oil. Add the spices into the bowl and coat evenly. Set aside while preparing the grill.

3. Preheat your gas or charcoal grill to medium-high heat.

4. When the grill is ready, at about 450 to 500 degrees with the coals lightly covered with ash, add the shrimp onto the grill and grill over direct heat. Cook until the shrimp are slightly firm and are opaque throughout. Remove from grill and let cool or 5 minutes. Serve warm.

1 tablespoon celery salt

¼ teaspoon cayenne pepper

¼ teaspoon paprika

¼ teaspoon ground allspice

1 teaspoon coarsely ground black pepper

½ teaspoon kosher salt

30 large shrimp, peeled and deveined

2 tablespoons olive oil

Onion-and-Garlic Smoked Mussels

Onion-and-Garlic Smoked Mussels

MAKES 4 TO 6 SERVINGS • ACTIVE TIME: 30 MINUTES •
TOTAL TIME: 1 HOUR AND 10 MINUTES

Mussels are great when flavored with some lemon and garlic. You can also pop them in Grilled Seafood Stew in Tomato Broth (page 250).

1. In a large bowl, combine the cleaned mussels, parsley, 4 garlic cloves, and olive oil and toss evenly. Next, squeeze the lemon halves over the mussels and then season with coarsely ground black pepper and sea salt.

2. An hour before grilling, add the yellow onion and 4 remaining garlic cloves into a bowl of warm water; let soak.

3. Preheat your gas or charcoal grill to medium-high heat.

4. When the grill is ready, at about 450 to 500 degrees with the coals lightly covered with ash, toss the soaked onion and garlic cloves over the coals, or into the smoking box. Wait 5 minutes for the smoke to develop (there will not be as much smoke as from traditional woodchips). Add the mussels into a grill basket (a sheet of aluminum foil will do) and place onto the grill. Cover the grill and cook for about 10 minutes until the mussels are opened.

5. Remove mussels when opened; for ones that haven't opened, try cooking them a bit longer and throw them out if they don't open. Transfer the mussels into a large bowl and let rest, uncovered, for 5 to 10 minutes before serving.

2 to 3 pounds mussels, cleaned and debearded

4 tablespoons flat-leaf parsley, chopped

8 garlic cloves, 4 minced

4 tablespoons olive oil

1 lemon, halved

Coarsely ground black pepper

Fresh sea salt

1 medium yellow onion, quartered

Grilled Whole Striped Bass

**MAKES 4 TO 5 SERVINGS • ACTIVE TIME: 30 MINUTES •
TOTAL TIME: 1 HOUR AND 30 MINUTES**

In the summer, I often try to catch a Striped Bass myself off our little Boston Whaler on the day of grilling. The Striped Bass is a very flavorful and fresh fish, so I recommend serving with a little fresh orange juice and some rosemary.

1. Grab the orange half and squeeze over the whole striped bass. Next, season with the rosemary leaves, coarsely ground black pepper, and fresh seat salt. Cover with aluminum foil and let rest at room temperature for about 1 hour.

2. Preheat your gas or charcoal grill to medium-high heat.

3. When the grill is ready, at about 450 to 500 degrees with the coals lightly covered with ash, place the whole striped bass on the grill for about 6 to 7 minutes, then flip. Finish cooking the fish for another 6 to 7 minutes, until the fish is juicy and opaque in the middle.

4. Remove the striped bass from the grill and transfer to a large cutting board. Cover and let rest for 5 to 10 minutes before serving.

½ **large orange**

**2 whole striped bass,
about 2 pounds each,
gutted, cleaned,
fins removed**

**2 sprigs rosemary,
leaves removed**

Coarsely ground black pepper

Fresh sea salt

Spiced-Honey Salmon

The sweet flavor of the honey pairs well with the fresh flavors of the salmon. Serve this with Charred Sweet Potatoes (page 259).

1. Combine the honey, chives, hot water, garlic clove, and lemon juice in a small food processor and blend to a paste. Remove the paste from the processor and coat the fillets evenly with the mixture. Season with coarsely ground black pepper and fresh sea salt. Set aside and let marinate for at least 30 minutes.

2. Preheat your gas or charcoal grill to medium-high heat.

3. When the grill is ready, at about 450 to 500 degrees with the coals lightly covered with ash, place the salmon fillets over direct-heat and cook for about 4 minutes per side, until the fish is flakey when pierced with a fork.

4. Transfer the honey-glazed fillets to a cutting board and let rest for 5 to 10 minutes before serving.

4 tablespoons honey

1 tablespoon fresh chives, chopped

2 teaspoons hot water

1 large garlic clove

½ small lemon, juiced

4 salmon fillets, about 4-inch squares

Coarsely ground black pepper

Fresh sea salt

Grilled Seafood Stew in Tomato Broth

MAKES 4 TO 6 SERVINGS • ACTIVE TIME: 45 MINUTES • TOTAL TIME: 1 HOUR

Always a favorite amongst seafood lovers, this classic dish tastes best when served in a tomato broth. Serve in large bowls and, if you would like, garnish with finely chopped, fresh flat-leaf parsley leaves. Place a bowl to the side for empty shells.

¼ cup olive oil

1 large shallot, finely chopped

4 garlic cloves, minced

¼ small green pepper, chopped

½ teaspoon dried oregano

½ teaspoon red pepper flakes

3 cups plum tomatoes, stemmed and crushed

2 tablespoons flat-leaf parsley, leaves removed

2 thyme sprigs

1 bay leaf

½ small lemon, juiced

2 cups clam juice

1 cup dry white wine

24 littleneck clams, scrubbed

18 mussels, scrubbed

14 large shrimp, peeled and deveined

10 2x1-inch pieces of striped bass

Coarsely ground black pepper

Fresh sea salt

1. Place a large Dutch oven on your gas or charcoal grill and prepare to medium-high heat. Leave the grill covered while heating, as it will add a faint smoky flavor to the skillet.

2. When the grill is ready, at about 450 to 500 degrees with the coals lightly covered with ash, heat the olive oil in the Dutch oven. Next, when the oil is hot, add in the shallot and minced garlic and cook for about 2 minutes, until the shallot is translucent and the garlic is golden, not brown. Add in the green pepper, oregano, and red pepper flakes and cook until soft, about 5 minutes.

3. Add the tomatoes, parsley, thyme, bay leaf, lemon juice, clam juice, and dry white wine and boil until thickened, about 15 minutes. Stir in the clams, mussels, and shrimp and cook until the shells open and the shrimp is firm. Add the pieces of striped bass and cook for another 3 minutes until the striped bass is opaque through the middle.

4. Remove the Dutch oven from the heat and season with coarsely ground black pepper and salt. Serve in warmed bowls.

Sides

If you don't take your grilling of fresh produce much far afield from kebab skewers, you're in for a major treat! We're going to walk you through how to grill everything from asparagus to zucchini.

My favorites include Grilled Beets with Walnuts (page 280) and Grilled Shishito Peppers (page 260), which are a bit of a flavor roulette because about one in ten is—yowza!—spicy! We'll grill tomatoes, scallions, eggplant, yellow squash, artichokes, broccoli, Brussels sprouts... basically, if it's a Paleo veggie, we've got a grill recipe that complements its unique flavor.

Sweet potatoes—unlike regular potatoes— are Paleo, and they're far tastier when charred on the grill than simply baked. Speaking of sweet, you've got to try our Grilled Pineapple Salsa (page 275), perfect for serving alongside seafood or chicken.

Grilled
Asparagus

Grilled Asparagus

MAKES 4 SERVINGS • ACTIVE TIME: 10 MINUTES • TOTAL TIME: 30 MINUTES

Often considered the ultimate side, grilled asparagus works well with virtually every dish.

1 to 1½ pounds fresh asparagus, washed

3 tablespoons olive oil

Coarsely ground black pepper

Fresh sea salt

TIP: IF YOU THINK EVERYTHING'S BETTER WITH BACON, TRY BACON-WRAPPED ASPARAGUS (PAGE 238).

1. Prepare your grill to medium-high heat.

2. Drizzle the olive oil over the asparagus and then season with coarsely ground black pepper and fresh sea salt.

3. Next, when the grill is ready, about 400 to 500 degrees, add the asparagus onto the grill. Turn the asparagus and grill until the asparagus are brown. Transfer to a large carving board and let rest for 5 minutes before serving.

Charred Sweet Potatoes

MAKES 4 SERVINGS • ACTIVE TIME: 45 MINUTES • TOTAL TIME: ABOUT 1 HOUR

Though they're most often baked, sweet potatoes taste even better and flavorful when grilled and charred. For a smoky flavor, consider throwing pre-soaked maple woodchips over the coals and grill with the lid closed.

1. Rub the sweet potatoes with olive oil and then season with coarsely ground black pepper and sea salt.

2. Prepare your gas or charcoal grill to medium-high heat.

3. When the grill is ready, about 400 to 500 degrees, add the sweet potatoes over direct-heat and grill for 45 minutes, turning every 15 minutes or so until finished—a fork should easily pierce through the sweet potatoes.

4. Remove from grill and serve.

4 large sweet potatoes
2 tablespoons olive oil
Coarsely ground black pepper
Fresh sea salt

Grilled Shishito Peppers

MAKES 4 SERVINGS • ACTIVE TIME: 10 MINUTES • TOTAL TIME: 30 MINUTES

This is one of my favorite sides, though often hard to come by. These peppers are best when charred and blistered. However, be careful, about 1 out of 10 are spicy!

2 to 3 cups whole shishito peppers
2 tablespoons olive oil
Coarsely ground black pepper
Fresh sea salt

1. In a cast-iron skillet, combine the shishito peppers and olive oil, and then season with coarsely ground black pepper and sea salt.

2. Prepare you gas or charcoal grill to medium-high heat.

3. When the grill is ready, about 400 to 500 degrees, place the cast-iron skillet on the grill and cook the shishito peppers in the skillet until blistered, about 8 to 10 minutes.

4. Remove from grill and serve immediately.

Grilled Cubanelle Peppers and Plum Tomatoes

MAKES 4 SERVINGS • ACTIVE TIME: 10 MINUTES • TOTAL TIME: 30 MINUTES

This mix of semi-spicy cubanelle peppers and hot, juicy tomatoes creates a truly flavorful side dishes.

6 cubanelle peppers

3 plum tomatoes, halved

2 tablespoons olive oil

Coarsely ground black pepper

Fresh sea salt

Sprig of rosemary (optional)

1. In a large bowl, combine the cubanelle peppers, plum tomatoes, and olive oil and mix thoroughly. Season with coarsely ground black pepper and sea salt and set aside.

2. Preheat your gas or charcoal grill to medium-high heat.

3. When the grill is ready, about 400 to 500 degrees, add the peppers and tomatoes onto the grill and grilled until charred, about 5 to 10 minutes.

4. Remove from grill, garnish with a sprig of rosemary if desired, and serve warm.

Grilled Scallions

MAKES 4 TO 5 SERVINGS • ACTIVE TIME: 10 MINUTES • TOTAL TIME: 20 MINUTES

Although this is a quick dish to make, it never fails to serve as a perfect side for steak or poultry.

1. Combine the scallions, lemon or lime juice, and olive oil in a medium cast-iron skillet. Season with salt and pepper and set aside.

2. Prepare your gas or charcoal grill to medium-high heat.

3. When the grill is ready, about 400 to 50 degrees, place the cast-iron skillet on the grill and cook the scallions until tender and charred, about 5 minutes.

4. Remove from heat and serve warm.

2 bunches scallions (about 15 to 20)
½ small lemon or lime, juiced
1 tablespoon olive oil
Fresh sea salt
Coarsely ground black pepper

Grilled Balsamic Peppers

MAKES 4 TO 5 SERVINGS • ACTIVE TIME: 15 MINUTES • TOTAL TIME: 30 MINUTES

The sweet and tart nature of this dish is perfect for a charred steak or pork chop. Also, with leftovers, consider making an open-faced steak sandwich topped with these peppers.

1. Combine all of the ingredients into a large bowl and mix thoroughly.

2. Place a cast-iron skillet on your gas or charcoal grill and prepare to medium heat. Leave the grill covered while heating, as it will add a faint smoky flavor to the skillet.

3. When the grill is ready, about 400 to 500 degrees, place the balsamic peppers into the skillet and cook until tender and lightly charred, about 7 to 9 minutes.

4. Remove from grill and serve with fresh arugula.

2 red bell peppers, stemmed, seeded and chopped into quarters

2 yellow bell peppers, stemmed, seeded and chopped into quarters

2 green bell peppers, stemmed, seeded and chopped into quarters

4 tablespoons olive oil

2 tablespoons balsamic vinegar

8 basil leaves

Coarsely ground black pepper

Fresh sea salt

Fresh arugula

Grilled Tomatoes with Garlic

Grilled Tomatoes with Garlic

MAKES 4 TO 6 SERVINGS • ACTIVE TIME: 15 MINUTES • TOTAL TIME: 35 MINUTES

Served chilled, nothing speaks summer like this side dish. Best when served with poultry or seafood.

10 whole tomatoes of your choice

4 large garlic cloves, chopped

¼ cup olive oil

4 chives, finely chopped

Coarsely ground black pepper

Fresh sea salt

1. Prepare your gas or charcoal grill to medium-high heat.

2. Stem the tomatoes, cut them into quarters, and put them in a medium bowl.

3. Add the garlic, olive oil, and chives, then season with coarsely ground black pepper and sea salt. Set aside.

4. When the grill is ready, at about 400 to 500 degrees, add the tomatoes onto the grill until skins are charred, about 5 minutes. Serve warm.

Grilled Yellow Squash

MAKES 4 TO 5 SERVINGS • ACTIVE TIME: 10 MINUTES • TOTAL TIME: 20 MINUTES

Grilled yellow squash is a summery complement to seafood dishes.

1. Prepare your gas or charcoal grill to medium-high heat.

2. While waiting, cut the squash diagonally into long, ½-inch slices. Add the squash to a small bowl and mix with olive oil, black pepper, and fresh sea salt.

3. When the grill is ready, about 400 to 500 degrees, add the squash slices onto the grill and cook, flipping once, until tender—about 10 minutes.

4. Remove from grill and serve warm.

Medium yellow squash

¼ cup olive oil

Coarsely ground black pepper

Fresh sea salt

TIP: CONSIDER DOUBLING THE RECIPE, ADDING A MEDIUM ZUCCHINI.

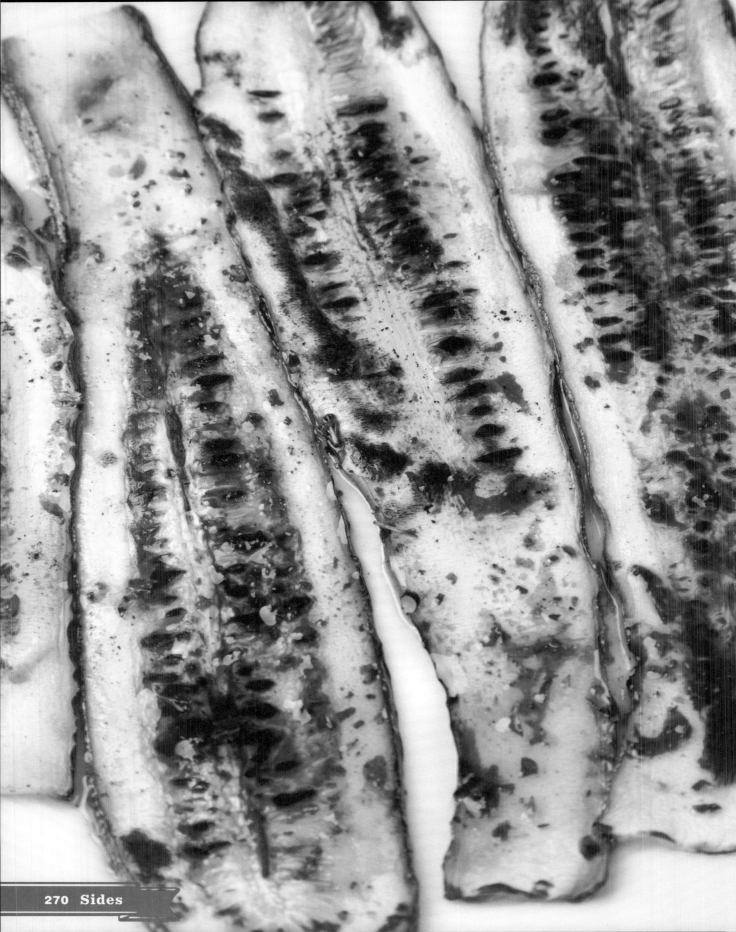

Grilled Zucchini with Sea Salt

MAKES 4 TO 5 SERVINGS • **ACTIVE TIME: 15 MINUTES** • **TOTAL TIME: 35 MINUTES**

When seasoned generously with a little lemon and some coarsely ground black pepper and sea salt, this grilled zucchini has surprisingly flavor.

1. Prepare your gas or charcoal grill to medium-high heat.

2. While waiting, toss the zucchini, lemon juice, black pepper, and salt in a small bowl and set aside.

3. When the grill is ready, about 400 to 500 degrees, add the zucchini to the grill and cook until charred, about 10 to 15 minutes.

4. Remove from grill and serve warm.

4 medium zucchini, halved lengthwise

¼ small lemon, juiced

Coarsely ground black pepper

Fresh sea salt

Grilled Eggplant with Herbs

MAKES 4 TO 5 SERVINGS • ACTIVE TIME: 30 MINUTES • TOTAL TIME: 45 MINUTES

This Italian-inspired dish can either stand on its own or be used as a side—though, be warned, it often steals the spotlight from the main dish.

½ **small white onion, finely chopped**

½ **cup olive oil**

¼ **cup parsley leaves, chopped**

1 **medium eggplant, sliced in half lengthwise**

Coarsely ground black pepper

Fresh sea salt

1. Combine the onion, olive oil, and parsley into a roasting pan and mix thoroughly. Next, add the eggplant halves into the mix and let stand at room temperature while you prepare the grill.

2. Prepare your gas or charcoal grill to medium-high heat. Designate two sections of the grill, one for direct heat and the other for indirect; you will want to cook the eggplant over indirect heat.

3. When the grill is ready, about 400 to 500 degrees, remove the eggplant halves from the roasting pan and place them down over indirect heat. Cover the grill and cook for about 15 to 25 minutes until softened.

4. Remove from grill and serve warm.

Grilled Artichokes with Garlic

MAKES 4 TO 5 SERVINGS • ACTIVE TIME: 25 MINUTES • TOTAL TIME: 45 MINUTES

Artichokes need to be softened up first in boiling water, but then they're perfect candidates for the grill. Their flavor is mild enough to be paired with a glass of white wine.

½ large lemon, juiced

3 large artichokes, trimmed and halved lengthwise

5 large garlic cloves, finely chopped

½ olive oil

Coarsely ground black pepper

Fresh sea salt

1. Fill a medium stockpot with water and lemon juice, and then bring to boil over medium-high heat.

2. Prepare your gas or charcoal grill to medium-high heat.

3. When the lemon-water is boiling, add the trimmed artichokes to the water and boil until tender, about for about 15 minutes. Drain and mix in a small bowl with the garlic, olive oil, black pepper, and sea salt

4. When the grill is ready, about 400 to 500 degrees, put the artichokes on the grill and cook until lightly charred, about 6 minutes.

5. Remove from grill and serve warm.

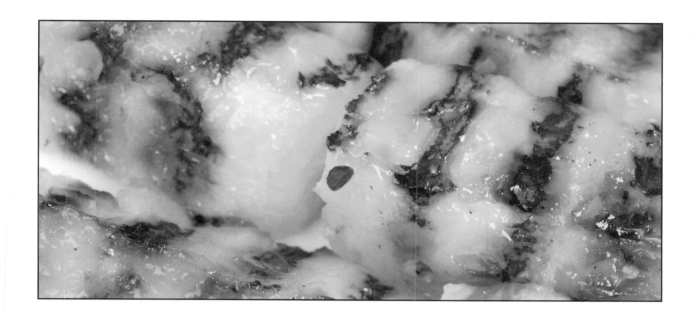

Grilled Pineapple Salsa

MAKES 4 SERVINGS • ACTIVE TIME: 15 MINUTES • TOTAL TIME: 30 MINUTES

Grilling brings out the flavor in the pineapple, pepper, and onion in this tasty cold salsa. Serve it alongside seafood or chicken.

1. Prepare your gas or charcoal grill to medium-high heat.

2. When the grill is ready, about 400 to 500 degrees, add the pineapple slices, red bell peppers, and red onion quarters onto the grill. Cook the pineapple slices until slightly browned, about 4 minutes, and then remove the pineapple and set on a chopping block.

3. Continue to grill the peppers and onion until charred, about 4 more minutes, and then remove and place on a chopping block.

4. Next, chop the pineapple, pepper, and onion into ½-inch cubes, and then transfer to a medium bowl.

5. Stir in the cilantro and lime juice, and season with coarsely ground black pepper and fresh sea salt. Serve chilled.

1 large pineapple, peeled, cored, and cut into 1-inch slices

1 red bell pepper, peeled and chopped into long strips

½ small red onion, quartered

¼ cup fresh cilantro, finely chopped

¼ small lime, juiced

Coarsely ground black pepper

Fresh sea salt

Grilled Broccoli with Lime-Butter

MAKES 4 SERVINGS • ACTIVE TIME: 15 MINUTES • TOTAL TIME: 35 MINUTES

Grilled broccoli with lime-butter gives off a soft flavor that will never overpower its main course. It's great alongside pork or poultry.

1. Prepare your gas or charcoal grill to medium heat.

2. Combine the clarified butter, lime juice, garlic, and cilantro into a small saucepan over extra-low heat and stir occasionally. Season with black pepper and sea salt.

3. When the grill is ready, about 400 degrees, brush the broccoli florets with olive oil and place on the grill. Cook until lightly charred, about 10 minutes, and then transfer to a medium bowl.

4. Remove the lime-butter from the burner and then mix with the broccoli florets. Serve warm.

6 tablespoons clarified butter

¼ small lime, juiced

2 garlic cloves, finely chopped

½ teaspoon finely chopped cilantro

Coarsely ground black pepper

Fresh sea salt

4 heads broccoli, stems trimmed and cut into florets

2 tablespoons olive oil

Grilled Brussels Sprouts

MAKES 4 SERVINGS • ACTIVE TIME: 10 MINUTES • TOTAL TIME: 30 MINUTES

Crispy on the outside and succulent on the inside, grilled Brussels sprouts go well with practically every dish. Consider serving alongside a steak and a glass of red wine.

2 cups Brussels sprouts, halved

3 tablespoons olive oil

1 garlic clove, minced

Coarsely ground black pepper

Fresh sea salt

1. Prepare your gas or charcoal grill to medium heat.

2. Combine the Brussels sprouts, olive oil, garlic, pepper, and salt in a large bowl and mix thoroughly. Then pour the contents of the bowl onto a large sheet of aluminum foil and roll up the edges as if to make a bowl.

3. When the grill is ready, about 400 degrees, add the aluminum foil bowl with the Brussels sprouts onto the grill, and then cover the grill and cook for about 5 minutes. Stir the Brussels sprouts and cook for a few more minutes, until lightly browned.

4. Remove from grill and serve warm.

Grilled Beets with Walnuts

MAKES 4 SERVINGS • **ACTIVE TIME: 20 MINUTES** • **TOTAL TIME: 1 HOUR**

Grilled beets are my mother's favorite side since the flavors are so rich that there does not need to be many to satisfy everyone at the table. However, be sure to wash your hands right after handling the beets as their violets tend to stain.

1. Combine the beets, walnuts, and olive oil in a large bowl and let rest for 30 minutes.

2. Place a medium cast-iron skillet on your gas or charcoal grill and prepare it to medium-high heat. Leave the grill covered while heating, as it will add a faint smoky flavor to the skillet.

3. When the grill is ready, about 400 to 500 degrees, transfer just the beets onto the grill; do not place in the cast-iron skillet. Grill the beets for about 10 minutes, until tender and marked. Transfer the beets to a large bowl and cover with aluminum foil.

4. Add the walnuts and oil into the cast iron skillet and cook until browned, about 2 minutes. Remove and mix in with the beets. Season with pepper and salt and serve warm.

6 medium beets, peeled and halved
½ cup walnuts
¼ cup olive oil
Coarsely ground black pepper
Fresh sea salt

Desserts

Embracing a Paleo lifestyle may require cutting out added sugar and artificial sweeteners, but it doesn't demand sacrificing sweets entirely. Paleo-friendly pastries and confections abound thanks to easy-to-make nut-based and coconut-based flours. But when it comes to the perfect way to top off a backyard barbeque, or the ideal dessert to accompany a hearty steak, I tend to seek out simpler, purer ingredients: fruit. Plus, if your grill is already hot, why not opt for dessert recipes that take advantage of those flames?

I've always considered fruit to be nature's candy—filled with natural sugars, they're certainly not lacking in sweetness. But unlike most other items that fall into the dessert category, fruit is nutrient-rich and bursting with fiber. These whole foods make for perfect Paleo meal-enders, especially during grilling season. Whether skewered and grilled, frozen into popsicles, or simply drizzled with raw honey, you won't find yourself craving sugar-laden desserts while enjoying the simple pleasure of a tantalizing bowl of grilled peaches and cream.

Just remember to buy local or organic fruit whenever you can. Make a trip to your local farmer's market and stock up on whatever produce happens to be in season.

Cinnamon Grilled Bananas

**MAKES 6 SERVINGS • ACTIVE TIME: 5 TO 10 MINUTES •
TOTAL TIME: 15 TO 20 MINUTES**

My first foray into grilling bananas was in the form of grilled fruit skewers:
I was at a backyard barbeque, and for dessert, the host had sliced up a
variety of fruit for everyone to poke with our bamboo skewers and roast over
an open flame. When heated, the bananas' natural sugars caramelized in
such a delicious way, I realized that they should be a stand-alone dessert unto
themselves. Sprinkle with some cinnamon, and you won't believe there's no
sugar added to this Paleo-friendly treat!

1. Clean your grill rack thoroughly, and brush lightly with coconut oil (the fruit will be placed directly onto the grill).

2. Wash and dry your unpeeled bananas.

3. Without peeling the bananas, trim the ends and slice them lengthwise, with the peels remaining on.

4. Bring your grill to medium heat. Grill your bananas with the fruit face-down (or, fruit-side down) over medium heat.

5. After about three minutes, when grill lines appear on the fruit, flip over the bananas and allow them to cook for a few minutes more, peel-side down. Allow the banana skins to grow dark.

6. Remove the bananas from the grill, sprinkle each with a dash of cinnamon to taste, and serve warm. Serve in bite-sized slices, if desired.

Extra virgin coconut oil, to brush the grill rack

6 large bananas, medium-ripe (preferably organic)

1 teaspoon cinnamon

VARIATIONS

- *Sprinkle with unsweetened coconut flakes instead of cinnamon to create a tropical flavor!*

- *If you have bamboo skewers handy, peel and slice the bananas into bite-sized chunks, and grill on skewers instead to create tasty banana kababs! Try alternating between pineapple chunks for a tropical flair, and finish them off with a sprinkle of coconut.*

Grilled Peaches with Coconut Cream

Grilled Peaches with Coconut Cream

MAKES 3 TO 6 SERVINGS • ACTIVE TIME: 30 MINUTES • TOTAL TIME: 35 MINUTES

This Paleo take on the classic dessert is surprisingly simple to make, and it proves just as satisfying as the dairy-and-sugar-laden version. Grilling the peaches enhances their tangy sweetness by allowing the natural sugars to caramelize, and the rich and silky coconut cream, plus a drizzle of honey and sprinkle of chopped nuts, makes for the perfect topping.

CREAM INGREDIENTS

13.5-oz can whole (or full-fat) organic coconut milk, refrigerated overnight

2 teaspoons raw honey (preferably organic), or pure maple syrup

1 teaspoon pure vanilla extract (or one vanilla bean)

TO MAKE THE COCONUT CREAM

1. Remove the can of whole coconut milk from the refrigerator and open the can. The liquid should have separated from the thicker, heavier cream.

2. Pour the liquid out of the can (and save it in a separate bowl—use it for a paleo soup or smoothie!).

3. Scoop the remaining cream into a bowl and whip it with a whisk until it reaches a consistency and texture like whipped cream.

4. Whip in the honey and vanilla; add more to achieve desired sweetness.

5. Put the bowl of prepared coconut cream in the refrigerator until the grilled peaches are ready.

TO MAKE THE GRILLED PEACHES

6. Start by washing your peaches and slice them in half, removing the pits.

7. In a small saucepan, combine the honey, clarified butter, vanilla, and salt over low heat and stir until the butter has melted and the ingredients have combined to form a light sauce, about five minutes. When the sauce starts to bubble, remove from heat and set aside.

8. Brush your clean grill rack lightly with coconut oil.

9. Bring your grill to medium heat. Place your peach halves face-down on the grill and drizzle with about ⅓ of your sauce.

10. Flip the peaches after about 10 minutes (or until grill marks appear on the flesh), and brush the surface with another third of your sauce. Allow to grill for another 5 to 10 minutes, or until peaches are tender.

11. Serve warm, topped with chopped pecans, a dab of coconut cream, and a drizzle of your remaining sauce.

GRILLED PEACHES

Extra-virgin coconut oil, to brush the grill rack

3 large peaches (preferably organic)

3 tablespoons raw honey (preferably organic), or pure maple syrup

2 tablespoons clarified butter or coconut oil

1 teaspoon pure vanilla extract (or one vanilla bean)

½ teaspoon sea salt

2 tablespoons coarsely chopped pecans, lightly toasted if desired

VARIATIONS

- *Top with any variety of toasted nuts or toasted coconut flakes.*
- *For a slightly tangier version, use nectarines.*

Grilled Watermelon Skewers

No dessert is easier—or healthier—than these grilled watermelon skewers. Juicy, fresh, and flavorful, these delightful kebabs embody the simple and carefree spirit of a backyard summer barbeque!

1. Cut your watermelon off of the rind and slice it into wedges that are about ½-inch thick.

2. Place three wedges each onto the bamboo skewers.

3. Brush your grill rack lightly with coconut oil. Bring your grill to medium heat.

4. Grill the watermelon skewers until grill lines appear, about two minutes.

5. Flip the watermelon skewers and grill the reverse side, about two minutes.

6. Squeeze some fresh lime juice over the watermelon skewers to taste, if desired.

7. Serve immediately, and enjoy!

Extra virgin coconut oil, to brush the grill rack

½ watermelon (or enough to produce about fifteen ½-inch-thick wedges)

Lime juice, to taste

5 bamboo skewers

Berry Parfait with Coconut Cream

MAKES 4 TO 6 SERVINGS • ACTIVE TIME: 10 MINUTES • TOTAL TIME: 15 MINUTES

This berry parfait recipe is, in a word, parfait (French for "perfect"). The coconut cream takes this deceptively simple fruit salad to the next level, and mashing raspberries into the cream itself makes for a rich, colorful presentation!

13.5-oz can whole (or full-fat) organic coconut milk, refrigerated overnight

2 teaspoons raw honey (preferably organic), or pure maple syrup

1 teaspoon pure vanilla extract (or one vanilla bean)

1½ cups raspberries, preferably organic

1 cup blueberries, preferably organic

1 cup strawberries, preferably organic

Fresh mint leaves, for garnish

TO MAKE THE COCONUT CREAM

1. Remove the can of whole coconut milk from the refrigerator and open the can. The liquid should have risen to the surface, separating from the thicker, heavier cream.

2. Pour the liquid out of the can (and save it in a separate bowl—use it for a paleo soup or smoothie!).

3. Scoop the remaining cream into a bowl and whip it with a whisk until it reaches a whipped-cream–like consistency and texture.

4. Whip in the honey and vanilla; add more to achieve desired sweetness.

5. Put the bowl of prepared coconut cream in the refrigerator.

TO MAKE THE BERRY PARFAIT

6. Rinse the berries and pat them dry. Slice the strawberries.

7. Scoop half of the coconut cream into a bowl, and mash in ½ cup of the raspberries until fully combined.

8. In a separate bowl, combine the remaining fruit.

9. In individual cups or jars, create berry parfaits by layering the ingredients: a layer of raspberry cream at the base, followed by a layer of fruit, followed by a layer of plain coconut cream, topped with fruit.

10. Garnish with mint, if desired.

Strawberry and Mint Salad

MAKES 4 SERVINGS • ACTIVE TIME: 10 MINUTES • TOTAL TIME: 10 MINUTES

I never considered combining mint with fruit until I tried a strawberry and mint salad at a family picnic. The flavors may not seem like a natural fit, but when combined, they complement each other in a refreshing way—like a mojito! If you forgo the drizzle of honey, this dish works well as a side, too, as it's not overly sweet.

1. Wash and slice the strawberries into quarters. Toss into a large bowl. Drizzle with the juice of one lime.

2. Sprinkle the mint over the strawberries, and garnish with an additional sprig of mint, if desired. Drizzle with honey, to taste. Serve, and enjoy!

4 cups fresh strawberries
1 lime
¼ cup fresh mint, torn
Honey, to taste

VARIATIONS

- *Add orange slices for a citrus twist, and drizzle even more lime juice, to taste.*

- *Substitute fresh two fresh basil leaves (thinly sliced) for the mint, and drizzle the finished project with lemon juice rather than lime juice, for an entirely different flavor combination that's just as tasty.*

Berry Delicious Popsicles

Berry Delicious Popsicles

MAKES ABOUT 10 POPSICLES (DEPENDING ON THE SIZE OF YOUR MOLD) •
ACTIVE TIME: 10 MINUTES • **TOTAL TIME: 3 TO 5 HOURS**

While your steaks are marinating, assemble the ideal summer dessert: fresh fruit popsicles! No baking, simmering, or grilling required—just assemble the ingredients, pop them into your freezer, and enjoy the results! Plus, the possibilities for variations are essentially endless!

INGREDIENTS

3 cups of your favorite berries
(I recommend blueberries
and pitted cherries)

¼ cup lemon juice

¼ cup raw honey

TOOLS

Popsicle mold

Popsicle sticks

Blender

1. Wash your berries and place them in your blender, along with the lemon juice and honey. Puree until smooth, about 30 seconds.

2. Pour into a popsicle mold and insert popsicle stick.

3. Freeze until popsicles hold firm (3 to 5 hours).

4. Briefly submerge the mold into lukewarm water. When the popsicles begin to separate from the mold, remove immediately. Pop the popsicles out of the mold, and enjoy!

VARIATIONS

* *Try adding in kiwi slices, pineapple, or other tropical fruit combinations for an entirely different flavor experience.*

* *Variation possibilities are endless. Enhance the flavor by adding any variety of "toss-ins," like fresh grated ginger, organic dark cocoa powder, pure vanilla or almond extract, unsweetened coconut flakes, or even sea salt!*

Piña Colada Popsicles

MAKES ABOUT 10 POPSICLES (DEPENDING ON THE SIZE OF YOUR MOLD) •
ACTIVE TIME: 10 MINUTES • **TOTAL TIME: 3 TO 5 HOURS**

It's the Paleo equivalent of an ice cream bar—but with the health benefits and robust flavor of creamy, delicious coconut. Cool down with this easy-to-make, Piña Colada–inspired, frosty treat!

INGREDIENTS

1 13.5-oz can whole (or full-fat) organic coconut milk

1 cup fresh pineapple, sliced into chunks

¼ cup raw honey

TOOLS

Popsicle mold

Popsicle sticks

Blender

1. Place all of your ingredients in a blender. Puree until smooth, about 30 seconds.

2. Pour into a popsicle mold and insert popsicle stick.

3. Freeze until popsicles hold firm (3 to 5 hours).

4. Briefly submerge the mold into lukewarm water. When the popsicles begin to separate from the mold, remove immediately. Pop the popsicles out of the mold, and enjoy!

Index

ABOUT CIDER MILL PRESS BOOK PUBLISHERS

Good ideas ripen with time. From seed to harvest, Cider Mill Press brings fine reading, information, and entertainment together between the covers of its creatively crafted books. Our Cider Mill bears fruit twice a year, publishing a new crop of titles each spring and fall.

VISIT US ON THE WEB AT
www.cidermillpress.com

OR WRITE TO US AT
12 Spring Street
PO Box 454
Kennebunkport, Maine 04046